For Sheila and Máire

'Far beneath the many thick layers of indoctrination
about who we are and who we should be lies an original
self, a person who came into this world full of possibility
and destined for joyful unveiling and manifestation.'

Thomas Moore, *Original Self*

Dear Reader

When my mother died, I was struck by all the care and attention her family (me included) paid to farewelling her. I knew almost straightaway I would want to record these cultural and personal tributes. Although I noted down some of the details at the time, it was not till a year after she died that I really started to write about my experience. I wrote about what happened and how I felt, much as I might have written a diary. Most of the words came naturally, and although some of the writing was painful, it was therapeutic to put it on paper and put it behind me. The writing process seemed to seal the events in the past and somehow enhance the present.

When I thought about publishing the words, I had to think of readers, and the extra details they (you) might need to complete the picture. While I want to tell 'the truth', there are many versions of it. I do not wish to portray my mother as an angel, nor do I feel the need to reveal all her demons. I see people as a multitude of often-fragile layers and I don't want to pin her down like a butterfly in a collector's drawer.

You have to remember that it's my view only; others may see things differently. And it's also the view that I am prepared to share. People asked me if it was difficult to write this book, thinking it would bring back unwelcome emotions. I didn't find that aspect hard, but writing about Mum's life was challenging at times. Memory is not reliable. It doesn't always yield the clarity you'd like. Sometimes, heading back into the past for some insight, I felt like I was in a dark wood, with a small torch for light. I could pick out only a few details, and could not always find what I was looking for. Also, for the sake of their privacy, I did not wish to write in any detail about some of the important people in my mother's life. Walking the tightrope between these constraints was what was difficult. But in the end, I had to remind myself that I was not a fact-hungry biographer ready to turn every stone in order to create the ultimate portrait or record. Mine is a more gentle and personal path. For now, this is what I can share with you.

Alison Haynes
Austinmer, 2007

ONE

WHITE BOUGAINVILLEA

Mum, it's been a few years now since you went.
This is how it happened.

The phone called out relentlessly into our dark and still little house in Sydney, piercing the silence and creeping into our dreams. Peter and I were curled up asleep upstairs on our futon, under the quilt, the boys in their red bunk downstairs. Who's calling at this hour? I thought sleepily as the ringing persisted. I reflected, somewhat irritated, that it could be my mother, who, like the rest of my family, lived in England, many time zones away from our home. It was warm in bed and I wanted more sleep. Maybe she's got the times muddled ... oh, whoever it is will call back if it's important ... I turned over, pulling the sheets up over me.

I let it go to the answer machine, resolving to call back

when it was light. But I still strained to hear if the caller left a message.

'Alison, it's Fiona. I need to speak to you. Can you call me as soon as you get this message.'

My sister's message was deliberate and paced, her voice steely but I thought I could detect a very slight trembling. She would have no doubt about the time here in Australia. Something was very wrong. I got out of bed immediately. I fumbled for my glasses, where I usually leave them just tucked under the wooden slats, but couldn't find them so ran down the stairs in a blur, my bare feet on the coir. I pushed the phone buttons for her number, holding my phone list up close to my face so I could read it. It was 4.29 in the morning.

When she answered the phone, Fiona's voice was a mix of businesslike and tired. 'Mum was found dead this morning,' she said.

I let out a sharp gasp.

Peter had come downstairs too, in his cotton dressing-gown and handed me my red one, and my glasses. I listened to Fiona explain the circumstances and mouthed to Peter, 'My mother has died.' His face fell and he hugged me.

Fiona had only just found out herself. A quarter of an hour beforehand. It was 7.30 or so in the evening in England and a village friend of Mum's had called her. The alarm had been raised some time after lunch. News travelled quickly in the small village and he'd been trying to get hold of Fiona all afternoon. She wanted to let me know as soon as possible.

From what we could gather, Mum had died in her sleep, in bed. She'd been ill for years and in some ways we knew it was on the cards sooner rather than later, but it was still a shock. I can't remember what details were discussed then—I knew she'd been found by the police, or was it the ambulance officers? There was talk of the police having taken her valuables—her purse and rings—and they were at the police station. It seemed strange that the police should become involved in a matter as simple as a sick woman dying in her home. But I guess it's not all chasing robbers. Over the next days and weeks the story of her discovery would become clear. But it's hard to remember what we said that early morning.

I walked into our terrace's tiny courtyard after putting down the phone. The papery flowers of white bougainvillea spilled over the shed, the jacaranda flowers were just beginning to bud. The sky was a gentle yellowy pink. It was cool.

In a phone call, the world had changed.

Peter made me tea. I cried and felt a flood and whirl of thoughts. I pictured my mother lying peacefully in her bed in the upstairs room of her lovely hundreds-of-years-old house, with the sun pouring in from the high street, the ancient wooden beams she liked so much, her ornaments.

An immediate thought was how glad I was that we'd so recently had the year in England and had seen so much of her. Again and again I felt so relieved we'd spent the time there, even though it had cost us our savings and we were still recovering financially.

I'd said goodbye to Mum on her drive behind the house on a cold March day, just seven months back. For the past few years each goodbye at the end of a visit was accompanied by the unsaid possibility that this was the last. But in a way, there'd been so many—when Harry, my eldest son, was one, two, three and then our arrival for a year. I still remember the pride and importance Mum relayed when a friend of hers said to me, 'And how long are you over for?' expecting the usual 'three weeks' or 'four'. 'She's over for at least a year!' Mum had said forcefully, as if it reflected well on her. Well, it did reflect well on her. I wanted to be there and spend more time with her. Although I hadn't made much of it, I had the uneasy feeling that we'd be able to afford it after she died, but what a shame that would be, I had thought, if we only got to live there again when she'd gone. So I did go back. We'd said so many goodbyes and each one was strongly underpinned by hope—that we'd see each other next time. But in the back of our minds, there was the constant knowledge that Mum was getting weaker, that miracles seemed to have happened already and that we couldn't expect many more of them. And at the same time, in this paradoxical world, the feeling that ... well, you just never know ...

When she died, there was almost a sense of discovery. 'So this is how the story ended.' As if, although we were part of the story of her life, we had no idea of the ending. We'd witnessed her failings, her illness, caused, we assumed by her drinking problem, been party to the tiny details of her life, the latest embroidery completed and hung on the wall, her sense of achievement when she managed to get a history class up and running in the village. How would her story end?

We sensed a sad ending, maybe even a gruelling one ... but as endings went for her story, she'd have liked this one. Mum had been ill for some time and we knew her hold on life was fragile, yet at the same time she'd seemed quite stable—carrying on with life: looking after a friend's dog, visiting another who had cancer, being thrilled about a new vase for the bathroom, getting ready for her next history class. There were so many ways she could have gone: getting weaker and weaker, spending months in hospital, with me wondering if I should fly over, Fiona spending weekends driving up and down from Devon. But this was how it ended. A normal day, a happy week and—bang!—the light went out. We knew that really it was a happy ending.

There were many phone calls in those early hours that morning. Calls to Fiona, to my dad, from whom she'd separated around six years before. I spoke to Sheila, Mum's youngest sister. She'd heard from Máire, the eldest sister (Mum was one of four, three girls and a boy, Jim). 'Are you sitting down?' Máire had said, 'Eleanor's dead.'

'She was my best friend,' Sheila told me that morning. 'My best friend.'

I tried to remember when I'd last spoken to Mum. The last call from her had been a week or so ago to say that Pudsey, Sheila's cat, had died. Sheila had lost her job too. As I had been visiting a friend, it was Peter who had spoken to Mum on that occasion. The last time I'd spoken to her was a week or two before that. She had been in good spirits, talking a lot about Clare, an elderly villager with children with incredible names. Mum was telling me about the son who had an unusual name, Wriley? Wrigley? And that was only one of them. He had about six names, almost all of them uncommon. She was interested in names and often scoured the births page in the paper and would cut out particularly ridiculous examples to send to me.

Sheila had spoken to Mum on the Sunday, and Mum had left Máire a message on her phone on Monday night, only days before she died. She was in really good spirits, sounded full of energy and happy. She was excited about a bit of gossip in the village—someone who'd set themselves up as high and mighty turned out to be on some sort of low-income benefit. Something like that. I never got to the bottom of it. Didn't really interest me. But the snobby streak in Mum was thrilled.

Another fairly recent conversation was the night before she turned sixty. She called me, it would have been late in the evening in England. She was worried about turning sixty and becoming officially a pensioner. She wondered if that changed anything—whether she was entitled to a pension, for instance—but didn't know how to go about even asking. I think she felt alone at times like that. She'd organised for Sheila, Máire, Fiona and her girls, Hope and Harriet—Mum's grandchildren—to come over on her birthday and they'd go out for lunch to a pub with a good dining room. There are some lovely old ones in the area and Mum knew her food.

The evening before her birthday she was feeling daunted

and not sure how she'd feel the next day. But she said she felt better after talking to me. I'd cheered her up. I can't remember what I'd said that had helped. I probably just listened. I said I'd call her the next day to wish her happy birthday. I did, and everyone was there. She was opening presents and sounded confident again. The little cup I'd sent her with butterfly wings for a handle had arrived without breakage. She was pleased I'd called, even though we'd only spoken the night before. It puffed her up a bit. There were some things right in the world—two sisters who visit on birthdays, a daughter who comes with her children and another who calls from the other side of the world to say happy sixtieth birthday.

The phone call from Fiona had come early on a Thursday morning in October. At first I thought I'd have to go back to England that weekend so I started to make plans and lists and pore over the decisions to be made. How long would I go for? A week? Two? Would I take the children? Not Harry because he'd miss school. Not Felix either, maybe? It would be a long way to go with jet lag each end. Not a great trip for a toddler. No, Peter would be coping on his own.

Only hours after the stony stillness of the news of death, life rumbled into action and the 'to do' list grew quickly: call the Flight Centre; call after-school care and fix up Wednesdays again as Harry's soccer practice was over for the year. This would give Peter more child-free time for work. Cancel today's meeting with my publisher. I called her extension early in the morning, knowing she wouldn't be there and left a message saying I'd had bad news and would have to fly to England; let a friend know I wouldn't be coming to the girls' night out next week; let the composting workshop know I wouldn't be able to attend; cancel tomorrow's interview; call the Writers' Centre and let them know I wouldn't be able to volunteer at the festival after all this weekend; buy a supply of knickers for the boys so Peter would not be stuck if he got behind in the washing ...

I needed to cancel dinner tomorrow night with some friends. We'd only asked one of them the night before. We'd taken sausages, crusty bread and tomato sauce to the barbecue at Moore Park. We'd drunk wine while the boys ran about, with and without ball. The friend had asked after my mother. 'She seems fine ... ' I had said, ' ... quite stable, though tired at times.' The sunset was beautiful that evening, behind the blue, white and red city lights in the distance, behind the expansive silhouettes of the Moreton Bay fig trees. Mum may even have been dead then, I thought later.

As soon as it was a decent hour I called our good friends, Bruce and Karen, who'd known Harry since he was a baby, to let them know that my mother had died and Peter might appreciate a bit of help at the weekend. Harry and their son, Max, were best of friends and attended the same inner-city school. 'Sorry, mate,' Bruce said to me in the playground a little later in the week.

I took Felix to day care as usual. Probably a bit late. Harry was late for school so we got a late note from the office and wrote 'family bereavement' for the reason. At day care I checked about fixing up an extra day, on Wednesday for Felix. There was a vacancy and I'd need it for my work, and it would make a lot of difference to Peter's coping when I was away. I also checked the possibility of extra casual days if Peter needed, explaining that I'd need to go to England because I'd had some sad news. 'Is someone ill?' Robyn, the day care coordinator, asked.

'My mother has died,' I replied.

She looked shocked. 'When?'

'I found out about four this morning,' I said.

'What are you doing here?' she asked. 'I'd be a mess if I'd only just found out my mum had died.' She gave me a hug, her eyes filling.

'Life goes on,' I explained. 'Especially when you've got children to look after.'

I'd always wondered how people managed to talk cohesively in grief—when on the TV, for instance. I learnt very quickly that for me, at least, it was possible in many ways to carry on. 'Without a hitch' would be an exaggeration, but I was surprised at how I was able to function: to make the phone calls, carry on with the shopping ... make plans. I carried a sorrowful weight around with me for days, but that didn't mean I'd burst into tears every time anyone asked me how I was, or if I told them about my mother's death.

With all the phone calls at odd hours because of the time difference between Australia and England, the household routine took a shaking and getting Harry to school on time was a bit of a challenge. It would only last a little while though, and it made me realise how hard it must be for those little things, life's everyday routine matters, to carry on when there's really big things going on in a family.

Grief was a private world. It was sad and at times fierce, but also tidal: while there were times alone I'd let myself feel its full force, and almost relax into the feeling of loss; there were other times where I could adopt a more matter-of-fact manner, feel very together and competent. One minute, a shop assistant (of course, having no idea of what is going on in your life) might ask breezily, 'And how are you today?' and for a split second you can honestly answer, 'Fine, thanks.' But turning your back, you feel suddenly sad again, remembering the weight you carry with you, the sorrow that you won't ever be able to see that grieved-for person again.

It turned out to be quite a few days before I flew back to England. As Mum's death was classed as 'sudden' she would have to have an autopsy. It seemed somewhat incongruous to say Mum had died suddenly. In some ways she had already been living on borrowed time: six years ago she'd been told she'd have one year to live unless she had a heart transplant. She'd responded well to drugs and seemed to have adapted, like a model patient, to her new situation. But she was not what you'd call a well woman.

Then there was the question of whether or not she could be buried, as she wished, at Burwash Church, in the East Sussex village where she'd spent the last six years of her life. And if not—she was hardly a regular churchgoer—what would we do? Fiona talked to the rector early on and we were all relieved that Mum could have her wish. She loved old things—cottages, stately homes, churches soaked in history in remote places or with special misericordes and the like. It was utterly fitting and another part of the happy ending that she could be buried in this lovely graveyard, where children run to and fro to the village primary school, cats roam among the yew trees, villagers and visitors alike walk through to the fields beyond with muddy dogs. She'd like it there. Within view is the village war memorial, and the pub. With its hanging baskets outside in the summer and blazing fire inside in the winter. Ceilings strewn with jugs, stirrups, dried flowers. Mum had had lunches there with grandchildren and sisters ... had a little glass of white wine too many on occasion. Hugging the hill that descends into the valley are some lovely thatched cottages. One was Clare's, her friend whose dog she'd looked after just days before her death.

In the days following Mum's death I found myself trying to piece together what had happened when in her last few years. It seemed important to retrace the steps that had got us to where we all were. I remembered the phone call, in 1995, I think, from my father saying he'd left Mum. It was a shock, but not entirely out of the blue. He was not proud of his news, but it was done and he needed to tell me. We didn't discuss why. It was obvious. The 'whys' belonged to different times and different questions—when had it all gone wrong? How had he stayed with her so long? Why had it gone wrong?

Dad's news was another one of those early-morning calls.

When you're separated by half the world from your family, you tend to get news, by phone at least, in the morning or evening. Never the neutral time zones of lunchtime, or early afternoon. Quite often dressing-gown time. I remember walking back upstairs to our bedroom—it was just before children—and sitting down on the side of our bed. 'My father's left my mother,' I told Peter. I felt weepy, which seemed out of place. I wasn't a small child contemplating the breaking up of my family life. Nor even a tender teenager. I was a grown-up woman, degree behind me, job, house, husband ... I didn't even live in the same country as my parents. But I still felt sad and tumultuous: for them, I guess; for my mother, now officially alone; for the bitterness of my father (at least he was with someone else, and would build a life with her). How was Mum taking it? Could she grow from it? It seemed unlikely. Would she look after herself better? Maybe. Would it force her to review her life? She would, but not necessarily in the light we all thought she 'should'.

Soon after that, one of those tiny windows of opportunity occurred with Mum when she spoke honestly about her feelings. She admitted the marriage had not been right for many, many years. But even then, there was no discussion as such, more a case of listening to what she had to say. I don't think she ever spoke about it again.

A couple of months after my parents split up I'd had the

good news that I was pregnant and we visited England and stayed with her at the house in Kent where they'd lived together. Initially Mum had said she wanted to stay there, despite the suggestion that Dad buy her a house. The separation was still very raw and I felt stuck in the middle in a very upsetting way. Peter worried that the stress was not good for the growing baby. Mum was not 'ill' then, but I remember going with her to Tunbridge Wells, a smart regional town in Kent, and her complaining of her legs and seeming a little breathless and tired at times. I wasn't sure what to make of it and played it down rather than making more of it. But looking back, she was obviously not in good shape then.

Months later she decided she'd move house after all and take the pick of the furniture. She found a cottage on the high street in nearby Burwash village. She and Dad had been living in Kent; this house, although only a twenty-minute drive away, was across the border, in Sussex. It was part of what used to be a sixteenth-century inn, The Swan Inn. Mum's new home was 'Cygnet Cottage'. Máire and her husband, John, made several trips down to help her with the unpacking, Dad put pictures up and the like. Some time after that we heard she was not well. She told us she had problems with her arteries and some swelling in her ankles, I think, but we didn't get many details.

Then came what I call her 'crisis' the following year. She was having trouble eating. People told her she needed to eat more, but during one phone conversation she told me in a rather pathetic voice how the previous day she'd eaten a boiled egg and half a slice of toast. That was all, and it appeared to be the norm. Then she had some sort of collapse and ended up in hospital for a month. We found out later that she'd almost died, that the doctors had hardly expected her to make the weekend. She was in hospital for her fifty-fourth birthday and was diagnosed with dilated cardiomyopathy; basically an enlarged and inefficient heart. The condition has a number of possible causes, including an infection, vitamin deficiency or alcohol abuse. Sometimes it's not clear what causes it. In my mother's case, doctors made it clear to my aunts that she needed to stop drinking and to eat properly. I don't know to what extent they confronted her with it and how she responded. She certainly never talked to me about her drinking or what had caused her heart problems, nor to anyone else that I know of.

When she came out of hospital there was a suggestion that she go into some sort of home. She couldn't walk far and was very weak. How else would she look after herself? But Mum fought that—quite rightly, I think, it would have literally killed her. Instead, small adaptations were made at her house in Burwash to enable her to live there independently: rails on the stairway, some enormous contraption in the bath, a fridge in her bedroom and so on. And she'd qualify for home help, a carer-cum-cleaner, who'd help her wash her hair and get out of the bath, and do some of the more physically demanding aspects of the housework.

In the days following Mum's death, I found many of her letters, and letters and faxes others had written about her during that time and before. It was very calming. When I read her letters, I could hear her voice and almost be in that time again, when she was still alive. I came across a fax I'd sent over the period she was in hospital—when we all hung on snippets of news and insights from doctors and nurses. On settling Mum into the house, the district nurse had told my aunts, 'You do realise she is very sick. She will die.' At the time I thought the statement verged on the ridiculous. Of course. We're all going to die. But I suppose it's a clue to just how sick Mum was and she wanted to prepare us. 'I'm racking my brain but I can't see a positive outcome to all this,' I wrote to my sister.

Yet here, in all the sadness of my mother's death, it appeared there had been a positive outcome after all. She'd come out of hospital, been prescribed a dozen or so drugs, told she had a year to live without a heart transplant, decided life was worth living and started living it again, albeit with limitations. She'd responded almost miraculously to the medicines, moving out of that critical band, and with a heart condition that saw only one in five survive five years, Mum had had another six years of life. And pretty good ones at that.

I didn't sleep very well the first few nights after Mum's death. It wasn't so much not sleeping but waking early—around 4 in the morning, several mornings in a row. I didn't mind too much. In fact, there's always so much to do in a household, and more again with all the travel and funeral arrangements, that I quite liked the extra hours of peace and quiet.

Fiona and I emailed each other and phoned a lot. She kept me in touch with every little detail. There were some silly ones like arranging insurance for me to drive Mum's car. While she was alive I had her permission and had borrowed it on several occasions. There was one holiday where she'd said I could borrow it for the length of a visit, then changed her mind and got stroppy about it. It must have been when she was quite sick and we believed she wasn't up to driving anyway. Looking back, she had probably felt bombarded and there wasn't much she could do to assert her independence, so maybe that was an inconvenient way of demonstrating it. But generally I could drive her car and it was no problem. Now that she was dead, though, I couldn't have her permission, could I?

There was a similar ringing round for contents insurance for Mum's house. It's quite a different matter insuring someone's goods once they've died and there's no one living there. The premiums go up and the periods they're willing to insure for go down.

Fiona drove up to East Sussex, to the house. She told me that Cygnet Cottage felt peaceful and all the signs were that Mum had had a normal last day. She said she sat on Mum's bed, 'had a chat with her pillow' and 'said everything I needed to.' She had to go through drawers looking for paperwork for the solicitors and banks, and told me she kept telling Mum that she wasn't prying but needed to look for all the documents. She explained in an email: 'It felt OK. Also sat and played some of her piano music (very badly but I thought she might laugh at it anyway.) Then said goodbye and said I would be back on Thursday. It felt very strange leaving the house, but I do feel she has gone elsewhere and quite happily ... '

I agreed to organise the order of service and choose music for the funeral: hymns and music for both the beginning and the end of the service. We thought Mum might have written down her wishes. Some years ago she'd talked about a gravestone—it appeared she might even choose one—but she stopped talking about it and must have finally baulked at the idea. All it seemed she'd put to paper was a wish to be buried in Burwash. Fiona continued to hunt through piles of papers thinking she'd come across some 'direction'. But no. In fact, I think we were relieved that she hadn't been quite that preoccupied with her death—she'd faced it, I know that, but she'd not yet planned it.

The previous Christmas Eve we were still in England. We lived in Devon for most of that year, but would visit Kent regularly. Often we'd break the journey and stay a night or so with Sheila in west London. That Christmas Eve, Peter, Harry, Felix and I called in on our way back from Sheila's. We'd had a fabulous lunch with friends in Kingston, coincidentally where my mother's married life had begun. We were due to see Mum that evening, just for a short while. We'd set off later than we'd planned and it turned out that Mum was tired and had called Dad's home where we were staying to say don't come, she'd see us on Boxing Day. But there we were. She was a little maudlin but by the end of our visit had summoned up enough cheer to say she was glad we'd come after all, that we'd raised her spirits—the boys entertained her with mock fighting and requests, as usual, to watch the Kipper video tapes she'd recorded for them and which they had for years asked to watch whenever we visited. She was listening to some sad but beautiful female vocal music on a CD, sitting slumped in her pink-and-white checked armchair, arms folded. 'I'd like this to be played at my funeral,' she said, looking directly at me. 'I want you all to be weeping,' she continued with a faint smile and a glint in her eye. 'I'm sure we would be,' I replied.

Mum had told her sister Sheila of the piece of music and her carer, Jackie, too, but no one remembered which track it was, or what it was, really. Sheila said it was on a CD called *Classics 2000*, which she had too. I'd already done some listening to my CD collection in search of suitable music and thought maybe a piece written by Hildegard Von Bingen might be right for when the coffin was brought into the church. Searing, simple music by an unusual and talented medieval woman enjoying belated and modest fame. I was working my way through the Celtic music I had on CD as I thought it would be good to acknowledge my mother's Irish heritage. (She was born in Ireland and had come to England as a teenager.) But I also thought I should at least try and track down the music I knew Mum had thought of. I asked in the local music shop but they didn't have the CD. So I looked it up on Amazon.com and found a listing of the tracks. Number nine, Sarah Brightman, 'Time to Say Goodbye', could be the one. Later on I phoned Sheila and got her to play it down the phone to me. Yes, that was it. The track was more contemporary than I'd remembered and I wasn't sure how it would sound in church but—it was Mum's choice, we were all sure of that. Fiona didn't know if she'd have time to hunt through Mum's CD collection to find it, so Sheila posted her copy to Dad's house. At least a small part of our goodbye to Mum would be as she'd wanted.

My tasks were minimal and restricted. Fiona had much more of an onslaught. She made contact with the solicitor, the bank and building society, the police, rector, the funeral directors, made arrangements for flowers—she decided on a massive arrangement from us all to go on top of the coffin—newspaper announcements (*The Times* and *The Daily Telegraph*; Máire arranged for some Irish papers). Almost every step of the way we discussed it—whether by email or phone. I wrote the notice for the papers. Place names not advised because of the problem of thieves knowing certain people will be out. We thought she might like donations to be made to the friends of the local doctors' surgery instead of flowers but I didn't want to write 'No flowers' as it seemed so cold and bordering on offensive if that's what someone wanted to do. Instead I said, 'Please consider a donation … instead of flowers.' Fiona had to choose the type of coffin lining. It all seemed pretty daft, she told me later, and some of the choices totally inappropriate—a black lacy lining was one option. Some of the choices seemed superfluous—does it matter what sort of handles are on the coffin that holds and will take underground the body of your recently deceased mother?

Fiona also had to choose clothes for Mum. We agreed she should be buried in one of her smart, 'going out' jackets. Red was a good colour for her, though becoming a bit harsh as she became sickly. But in her last years especially, on the days she made an effort and went out for lunch, she often wore red. With some make-up, red lipstick and a burst of energy, she brushed up well. So, we agreed on a jacket and skirt, not a suit, but something nice. Fiona polished a pair of shoes for her, and picked out new underwear and tights from the supplies in the wardrobes.

We discussed what we'd wear too, for her funeral. 'Got to go and buy coats for the girls to wear to Mum's funeral,' Fiona ended one email, 'I don't think Mum would like them turning up in their waterproof kagouls.' I had a good black pleated skirt that I'd wear with a Chinese-style blue-and-black silk top. But I'd need a warm jacket too.

There was a Jaeger jacket Mum had bought me more than twenty years ago that I'd never worn, nor thrown out. We'd got it at a factory seconds shop and somehow it had never been quite right for any phase I was in. Too hot for Australia and too smart for the times I'd been in England on holiday. I'd had it dyed from bottle green to black in the hope I might find a use for it. It seemed just right for Mum's funeral.

In the daily discussions and emails Fiona and I swapped stories of how well we did or didn't sleep, or how we were bearing up physically. Fiona said her whole body was aching during these weeks—mind you, there was quite a physical element to much of what she was having to do. Lots of running around on errands and driving up and down between Devon and Kent and Sussex. Her legs in particular were quite painful. I, on the other hand, had what I described as a lozenge of pain at the bridge of my nose, just above my eyebrows. It was a spacey time. In some ways I felt we were on automatic pilot, going through the motions of what needed to be done, yet another part of me yearned to turn back the clock just a week or so before, to when Mum was alive. I was so far away from 'the action'. I wanted to plough my energy into tasks to help, but there was a limited amount of things I could do from

Australia. Mum was on my mind all the time; in fact, my thoughts were so much in England, with my sister, my aunts, the thought of my mother, her house, that sometimes I'd hear Tony Blair, the British prime minister, on the radio and half think I was in England.

It had only been a matter of months, after all, since we were there. We'd been on/off talking about going to England for years. Every now and then, when we got itchy feet, we'd talk about moving, the pros and cons of various options in Australia: round the corner in inner-city Sydney, the Blue Mountains, the Southern Highlands, Yarramalong Valley near Wyong where some good friends lived ... And we'd come back to England. We'd plan, look at house prices, rental prices. We seemed to be on our way once then Peter got cold feet. A few years later he had a conversation with someone in the internet travel business. They were talking of setting up in Cambridge, England and would Peter be interested in working for them? Would he what? We hardly took it seriously as it seemed so unlikely. It was by no means the first time someone had talked to Peter about him being part of big plans—and they didn't usually come to anything. But the subject came up again a few months later and a few months later again Peter was signing a contract that involved writing while still Sydney-based, then being transferred to Cambridge.

Peter had some very busy months—it was the year 2000, and Sydney was hosting the Olympics—and a few months more, lo and behold, we witnessed what was quickly labelled the bursting of the dotcom bubble. Suddenly internet businesses were no longer unquestionably viable and the travel company's plans changed. They dropped the idea of sending Peter to the UK. But we had not dropped it. Our lives were centred on that aim. We'd spent money on the house so we could rent it out, and I'd given my notice on some regular work I was involved in. There was talk about getting us over anyway, despite the change in plans. It was dragged out and out. We were in Sydney for the Olympics, which we hadn't expected to be (and hadn't expected to enjoy, but did) but eventually the company came good. The job wasn't there but the plane tickets for all of us were, and help with moving household goods. We decided we'd go to England anyway.

I lost a stone in weight planning our move. Felix, our second child, was less than eighteen months old. We had a house jammed with junk that needed sorting. My days became full of sorting, packing, taking bootloads of old toys, clothes, useless market finds to St Vincent de Paul. I hauled cheap furniture out of the house—stuff I'd never liked, there wasn't room and here was the perfect excuse—and left it on the street corner. It was usually gone within the hour.

Mum had enjoyed hearing about our progress. She checked through her bills and gave us breakdowns of expenses, to help us with our plans. She sent local papers with real estate ads so we could get an idea of rental costs. It was a huge upheaval, but so worthwhile. We'd spent a few months in Kent, then had rented a cottage in Devon, a drive that took between three and six hours to Kent depending on the traffic. One of the many good things to have come out of that year in England had been the realisation that even though I lived on the other side of the world, I'd not missed out to the extent I imagined when it came to spending time with my mother. I realised that each time I had visited, since I made a point of seeing her so often, we'd managed to spend a good deal of time together.

She'd been too sick to travel to our cottage in Devon, but liked to see photos of the quarter-acre garden, with its apple trees at the bottom and Peter's vegetable crops in the middle. She enjoyed the stories of pheasants wandering through the flower beds, and the badgers who stole Peter's corn. Harry told her about his new school, with just thirty-eight children. In the end we chose to live in Devon because it is so green and beautiful, rent was cheap as it was a distance from London, and because we knew three people living there: my sister, an old university friend of mine, and Peter's oldest friend, who had moved there from New Zealand. Mum liked to hear about the things we did together. We'd found a semi-detached Victorian farm cottage, surrounded by fields, a mile out of a tiny village called Yeoford. The village had all you needed: a pub, a train station (you had to hail the train to stop), a post office and village shop.

I loved being back in England, reacquainting myself with the names of all the wildflowers and trees of my childhood. I had hoped to go for a few years, but it proved hard to make new contacts for work, so we decided it would be a one-year adventure. When I left the village after the final cleanup at the cottage, a harvest moon, like an orange pumpkin, rose in the sky over the humped, thatched roofs, and for the first time ever in my life, I saw a badger trotting heavily along the lane side.

Mum was on my mind a lot. Sometimes it felt like a thick soup in there: thoughts swirling and churning. Every now and then a nub of truth would bubble up like a dumpling: I thought about her behaviour, how she'd treated us at various times of our lives. It wasn't that she was not kind. She had a great capacity for thinking of others. But she had a problem with intimacy. It explained a lot. Why she cut friends off. She didn't have many old friends, and in the last years had shut out the three or so people she'd known since I was a baby. Why her marriage had finally unravelled. Appearances were very important to her, but perhaps sometimes, for whatever reasons, she didn't follow through with the real stuff. Perhaps she had been in some ways 'unformed' when she started married life, and this had affected the dynamics of the relationship, and the way they communicated. The fact that Fiona and I often felt she didn't want to listen to us but preferred to ramble on about things which at times seemed trivial. She was proud, too.

The police very quickly found Mum's will. She'd sent Fiona and me copies and discussed aspects of it at great length. She went through a period, some time, even years after her 'crisis' of getting her will organised. Prior to that, she had the standard spouse's will which left everything to her husband. It took her several years to change her will. Perhaps, despite the separation, she had taken comfort in that legal link.

When I received a copy of her will I wrote to her saying I hoped it would sit in a drawer for many years to come. And I suppose it did. Another four years, anyway. On the visit after receiving her will, I remember her suggesting I look around and make a note of anything I'd like. I didn't.

But now it was up to my sister and me to deal with her house and its contents. The plan was that, over in England, Fiona and I would go through Mum's house and put aside things we wanted to keep, or could find good homes for, and a house clearer would do the rest. At some stage over the years Fiona had talked with Mum about her piano and was going to have that.

The only thing I'd ever allowed myself to think about having if and when Mum died was a painting of two small boys on the beach, digging in the sand. They are against the light and a wave laps gently around their feet. It has an ageless quality. It could be 1930s or 1990s. It could even be my boys. I said quite early on to Fiona that I'd like the painting of the boys; it was a symbol for me of continuity. I had always admired the painting, whether it hung in the house that my parents had shared, or at Cygnet Cottage in Burwash. The fact that it was the one thing I had given myself the freedom to covet linked for me the time before Mum's death and now, afterwards.

My boys were concerned for me, being so sad. But I assured them I wouldn't be sad forever. I told them it was normal to be sad and to cry when someone you loved very much died. I told them it was a good thing for me to cry, but it didn't mean that I felt sad all the time. Harry said he'd miss me while I was away, but he would be all right. Felix looked at me with concern from his little stroller throne:

'I'm sad because my mother is gone,' I told him.

'You lost your mummy,' he replied, sympathetically.

'Yes.'

'It's all right … she'll come back!' he assured me.

We talked about what it meant to die. And in another conversation, Felix seemed to have grasped the concept a little more.

'Your mummy's gone?' he asked me.

'Yes.'

'She's dead. She can't talk.'

'No.'

'But,' he pointed out more brightly, 'your daddy's all right!'

'Yes!'

My father organised a ticket for me to travel back to England. It was another two weeks before I made the trip as, although the autopsy was completed, the church was booked out.

Peter and I made wills before I left. We asked our neighbours to witness them. I wrote a letter to the boys in case something happened to me and dug out a photo of me that Peter could show Felix. Peter had made the reverse journey at the beginning of the year. We were still in Devon and his father had gone into hospital with bad stomach pains. He'd been active up to the last, hanging pictures, interested in Peter's news, but a few days later he'd died. There'd been updates, reports on his progress after surgery, good news, not so good, then it all seemed to crash and he was gone. So Peter had made his sad trip from the UK to New Zealand. Three days' travel each way. He was away a total of three weeks. While he was gone, we'd found a picture of Peter at some function or other, in his suit, smiling, and Felix would say, 'He's smiling at me,' which he liked the idea of.

I'd been slightly annoyed at Mum for not being more sympathetic about Peter's father's—Harry senior's—death. She'd rung me and rattled on in her usual manner about something or other and I'd hardly been able to get across our most urgent news. She took news of death in quite a matter-of-fact way in some respects. I think she was aware how close to it she was herself. At times she talked with sadness about a friend's death—Jean Maude Roxby, a wrinkled character who lived over the road in a magnificent old beamed house with views into the valley, and who'd known Rudyard Kipling as a child—or Hazel, whose cancer galloped onwards and engulfed her not that long after learning about it. There was a commonality in their illnesses, and a link between Mum and Dad since Hazel and her husband knew them both and were two of the very few people who Mum kept in touch after she and Dad split up. News of Princess Diana's death was a shock for her, given the fact that it came soon after Mum had received her prognosis of a year to live without a heart transplant and yet here was someone full of health and wealth and they'd died.

'Yes, the death of Diana was shattering,' Mum had written to me.

I turned on the radio in the kitchen on Sunday and instead of the usual programme, the announcer was talking about 'the loss of this young life.' I wondered who they were talking about and eventually it became clear. I was absolutely stunned. It was just so unexpected. I know that most accidental deaths ARE, but somehow I couldn't believe this one. Then the phone rang and it was the gas man—back to reality.

But Mum had sent a very nice card to Jan, Peter's mother, something to do with a climbing rose squeezing through the wall and onto the other side. She'd given it to someone else who really appreciated it, so had got a few 'in case'. Jan told me she gave the card pride of place.

The year had a sad symmetry for us. I was about to make my own heavy journey in the opposite direction to Peter's.

Before leaving I left Peter a 'guide' for looking after the boys. What days Felix went to day care, what he needed to take, when you needed to pay. What the lunch routine was with Harry, what to make for his packed lunch. I also wrote out a list of all the phone numbers that might be needed while I was away; school, day care, after-school care, friends who could be called on to help, the doctor, Harry's violin teacher, emergency numbers, numbers where I might be contacted in England, at Fiona's, at Sheila's and at Dad's.

I also wrote another list entitled 'Survival Notes' that I pinned on the noticeboard by the phone. Peter told me he referred to it often. Point number one, in felt tip: *Remember you're the best people in the world!!*

There was a summary, state of the art, of where Felix was in potty and toilet training—what to ignore, what to definitely not ignore, when to encourage, when not to worry. And, as I didn't want to have to start again on my return, instructions to under no circumstances put a nappy on him, even at night.

Under the heading 'Routine', I wrote: 'If you are not coping well with tired kids—get them to bed early (if necessary all go to bed in our bed). This means bath etc. early, e.g. eat 6–6.30, bath and pjs 6.45–7, book and bed 7.30–8.'

Day care goodbyes: 'Felix may be reluctant to let you go when you drop him off but be assured he recovers VERY quickly and proceeds to have a lovely day. Best to stay a little while then make a decision to go, leave him in the care of someone and GO.'

There were meal ideas, including a pretty comprehensive list of what foods the children liked, what vegetables they ate, which fruits. The minutiae of a parent's care.

Later in the week, I had my hair cut. I remember sitting there feeling sad and exhausted, Mum's death hanging there, but not really wanting to say anything or explain, yet at the same time feeling very quiet, not wanting to chat and feeling like I must be coming across very flat. Perhaps I should have said, 'I want you to cut my hair for my mother's funeral, I just found out a few days ago that she died and I've got to go back on Saturday,' but instead I just asked my hairdresser to do a gentle trim, nothing too drastic please, just a tidy-up, and left it at that.

I was sometimes surprised by people's reactions to my sad news. One day I met on the street someone I'd worked quite closely with. She asked how I was and when I said I was heading back to the UK for my mother's funeral, she looked very uncomfortable. She couldn't wait to get away. Other people were really supportive and happy to hear about how the various arrangements were going. A friend who'd grown up in a boys' home asked me what it was like to lose a mother. I think he was surprised I could hold a conversation together. Not ever knowing his, he said he didn't know and wouldn't know the grief of it. 'Maybe you've been grieving for her all your life?' I said.

In addition to seeing Mum's face a lot in my head, I had a number of dreams about her. In one of them, in the first few days after she died, there was a message on my answer phone. I could tell it was her voice but it was very, very faint. I could barely make out what she said. I had to play it several times to catch her words. She said, it seemed to be by way of explanation of why she'd gone, that she was very tired ... just very tired.

Another dream, a little later on, was of a beautiful lake scene, softly rippling water and a gentle blue-and-apricot sky. There was my mother, floating out into the distance—in a coracle. A coracle is a round Celtic boat, an ancient little boat the shape of a half walnut shell. It bobbed about, she holding the sides, circling just a little as it caught a current, a little like an upturned umbrella. It was old and worn. When I woke from my dream, I knew it was a coracle I'd seen. It's not a word I can ever remember using or particularly coming across, and I can't remember ever seeing one in my waking life. But coracle it was, with my Irish mother inside it.

In the early days after Mum's death, I had a strong feeling of love for her and it was painful that I felt it had nowhere to go—Mum was not there to receive it anymore so all that love couldn't be channelled. I felt like I wanted to hug her, and hug her often—I imagined my spirit embracing hers, or holding her hand. Sometimes in a beautiful garden inside my mind, green and dappled with bowers of white flowers. At the same time I was acutely aware that she'd never been a huggy sort of person when alive, and we didn't have that comfortable physical relationship some mothers and daughters do. My own sentimentality made me laugh and

I'd remember her matter-of-fact way of dealing with a lot of things—like a friend's death, or even her own state of health. If our spirits did meet—if there was life after death—we wouldn't hug any more than we did in this world. She'd tell me about her neighbours, she might make a nice lunch from a recipe she'd cut out and had been meaning to use, she might irritate me for not asking about my plans ...

Writing the words I'd say at Mum's funeral, I wanted to somehow put her death in greater perspective. 'I'd be happier if she'd got to seventy,' Fiona had said. Seventy years seemed 'respectable'. 'I always think of your mother as tragic,' a friend's mother said. I fought that one. Not tragic. No.

'I've done everything,' she said to me once in her little sunny sitting room.

I had felt impatient. 'What do you mean? You've climbed Mount Everest?'

'I've been to Wimbledon, Covent Garden ... '

I don't even remember where else she mentioned. She was talking about The Corporate Wife. As Dad had steadily gained promotions and become a senior executive in the oil industry, she had enjoyed the trappings: the invitations to

London and county events. She was very proud to have done these things. 'She led a very privileged life,' said her sister. The fact she thought she was lucky helped. I didn't want a tragic mother.

Comparing her death with Peter's father's earlier in the year I felt sad that she was only sixty, happy that she'd died a peaceful death at home. Harry senior, on the other hand, had reached the riper age of eighty-four but the last few days were full of hospital stress, tubes, emergencies and worry.

It was true, Mum had had lots of opportunities. She'd travelled, lived a comfortable life. It wasn't a perfect life, but whose was?

Saying goodbye to the boys when my taxi arrived for the airport was dreadful. It almost seemed worse than hearing the news that my mother had died. I'd got them each a little bag of goodies—some mouse and cat masks, new pens and drawing pads and so on. Felix told me he didn't want me to go. They were sitting on the stairs wearing the little masks, like furry glasses. I couldn't speak. 'Bye, Mummy!' I gave them a kiss each and made a dash.

T W O

FROM IRELAND TO ENGLAND

My mother was Irish, though you probably would not guess from her accent. She wasn't particularly interested in her family history, nor Ireland; she had other fish to fry.

My mother, Eleanor Clare McGonigle, was born in Drogheda. That's on the east coast of Ireland. She was born in 1942, although somewhere there is, or was, perhaps it's now lost, a birth certificate with a different year, produced in an Irish muddle over a passport when she was still living at home. That's the Irish for you.

But it was in 1942 that she came into the world. She was the second child in the family. Her sister Máire was three and a half when she came along. Their dad was Seamus. We used to call him Grandpa Mac—but that was many decades later. Their mum was Sheila. She came from a big family; she was one of fourteen.

When I knew them as my grandparents, Seamus was a talkative character in black round-rimmed glasses, with a rich Irish accent and an elaborate wiring system for his radio and hi-fi to match. Sheila—Granny Mac—was a gentle soul, who seemed happy with the quiet life.

After Eleanor was born, there was James (known as Jim) and Sheila, nicknamed Sheedy, to differentiate her from her mother. Sheila's twin brother, Patrick, did not survive long after his birth, despite being, at 3 pounds, half a pound heavier than his tiny sister.

A few years after the children were born, the family moved to Ballyshannon, which is on the other side of the country, on the north-west coast. The river there, the Erne, was being dammed, and a new hydroelectric power station was being built, so the little country town was experiencing a boom, what with all the construction workers and engineers involved in the various schemes.

Seamus's mother, Mary McGonigle, had been a widow for some years. She still ran the town drapers, but business was slowly declining. Seamus planned a new shop he called Electrical Contractors, where he'd sell radios and other appliances as well as do wiring contracts and electrical repairs. The family moved into the rooms above the shop.

It was a comfortable life. They weren't rich, but neither were they poor. They had young girls as maids to help out in the house sometimes, but didn't have a garden.

Grannie McGonigle, as Mary was then known, came in with Seamus when they moved. She was old by then. She always dressed in black, so Eleanor and the other children thought she looked like a witch and were scared of her. They took meals into her room on a tray, but when they put it down they ran out as fast as they could.

Seamus and his brother Pat inherited some money and decided to put it into building a cinema in Ballyshannon. They called it the Abbey Cinema and did a lot of the work themselves. Seamus spray-painted the rough-cast interior walls and when Máire returned in 2003, she could see his writing still on the wall above some old fuse boxes. Pat was the manager and Seamus was a projectionist. They had a huge row over money, however, and Pat left the town. They didn't speak to each other for years.

Seamus's word was law. It was like that in many Irish families. The father's word was law and there was no discussing it. Seamus was strong-willed, but by no means unique among the men of his generation. He loved fishing and mucking about with radios. Sheila liked to sit doing embroidery or knitting, or making raffia bags or rag rugs.

These were the early days of television. And soon Seamus

was right behind it. He became fanatical about trying to get a signal from the nearest transmitter in Yorkshire, on mainland England. The McGonigles were one of the first in the town to have a television set. When they put one in the shop window, it made the local paper. 'Many townspeople have been able to view television nightly in one of the windows of the Castle St Radio Store. Reception and sound are excellent,' enthused the *Donegal Democrat* of 18 November 1955.

I have this image of people wrapped up in thick coats standing in a huddle outside Grandpa Mac's shop window. It would have been pretty cold in November in Ireland. I wonder what they watched?

Although I don't think the McGonigles were overly religious, there were lots of nuns in the extended family, including many aunts. Every Sunday afternoon, three or four nuns from the local convent would come round to watch the family television. They watched a program called Life of Christ, even if the picture was all snow.

The girls went to the Convent of Mercy School in College Street (there was no choice). There wasn't a uniform, but Sheila remembers she was once sent home to change because Granny Mac had dressed her in trousers because it was so cold. Sheila was glad because there wasn't PE or outdoor sport, no school dinners either. I never knew anything about the school from my mother, but Sheila remembers distinctly that they were taught to knit 'small socks'.

I imagine Eleanor, maybe about seven or eight, walking at a smart pace down the pavement, maybe a school pack on her back, neatly dressed, socks pulled up, perhaps hands in pockets against the cool of an autumn morning. I imagine she would have been happy to go to school. She was a good student. I think she would have done her best handwriting and listened to the teachers.

A few lessons were in Gaelic and sometimes she and Máire went to the Gaelic summer school, but I don't think she remembered much.

They would have had their first Holy Communion at about age seven. It was the tradition in their family to wear their mother's wedding dress; presumably a cut-down version. It was considered a normal thing to do, but some girls got new dresses, sometimes even from America, which I imagine might have stirred up some feelings of envy.

Eleanor had piano lessons and used to enter competitions in nearby towns. I think she won some too. I have to confess, rather guiltily, that I never thought she was a very good piano player as an adult—perhaps she stiffened up. In any case, she went for years without playing. Maybe she never quite got her knack back.

Sheila tried piano lessons too, but after the first few lessons was sent home with sore, rapped knuckles and a note to her parents that they were wasting their money.

From a young age, Eleanor liked to befriend children from rich families. She also liked to act and, like others in her family, was often involved in the town shows.

I've got a newspaper clipping with a photo of a production of *Zurika* in 1950. There's Eleanor. One of nine little girl dancers dressed in floaty white dresses, patent leather buckle shoes and ankle socks, with flowered headdresses and a rope of flowers strung among them. She has a lovely, fresh face with a tentative smile, ears that stuck out just a bit, a lean little girl, standing straight, with feet together.

I love that look on her face, so many years ago. When it felt simply exciting to dress up and be part of a big show and have a photographer come and take your picture. That time in your life when you feel so important, when you really feel you are a pearl in the oyster world. And you *are* a precious pearl.

About the only thing I remember my mother telling me about life in Ballyshannon was that when they had nothing better to do she and her friends would dare each other to knock on doors and ask if they had a 'body'. That meant a deceased person laid out for a wake. If they did, the children would go into the house and sit quietly for a little bit and maybe pretend to pray, sometimes barely holding their sniggers. When Mum told me of it, when I was a girl myself, I thought it very strange. Later, I regarded it as healthy that children were allowed, maybe even encouraged, to confront death and see a corpse. It reminded me of the scenes in Huxley's *Brave New World* where children visit hospital wards as part of their education.

Sheila gave me a rounder picture of their childhood as she remembered it: games of hopscotch and skipping. Walks to the Mall Quay where you could look at the Inis Saimer island and the estuary, or further afield to the abbey well, where people tied pieces of cloth on a nearby tree as votive offerings to St Patrick. When I come across details like this, I'm struck by the foreign land that is my mother's childhood: the Catholic practices, the nuns that would come and watch telly, the hum of small business in the background.

Sometimes the family would drive to Bundoran (where Sheila senior and Seamus had met on holiday), looking out for fairy rings. Sometimes they'd take the train. Once there, they'd enjoy the beach, making sandcastles and riding donkeys. To me it seems odd that they weren't taught to swim. Perhaps there were too many obstacles; maybe there wasn't a pool in Ballyshannon then and the sea seemed too cold and rough, and the opportunities too short?

Often they'd stay in the caravan Seamus built at

Rossnowlagh, a short drive away on the coast. (It would have been built to last. When later he built a clothesline in the London garden, he gave it such solid foundations it took days to pull it out decades afterwards.) They would fish, or run in and out of the waves, or perhaps go winkle-picking and collect shells. At Loch Linchin and Loch Melvin, they'd go out in the dinghy. Later on, they'd cook the fish over a turf fire, and Sheila ('Mammy' as they called her) would boil a kettle. I love that image of the kettle over the turf fire. It makes Granny Mac seem earthy, which I don't really think she was. It's all much more idyllic than I had ever imagined their life to be, but perhaps that's because people have only told me, or written down the good bits.

There were picnics and occasional trips to Dublin to look at the shops. Several photos show the three girls dressed up for an outing to Dublin. Eleanor looks thirteen or fourteen perhaps. She and Máire wear tailored wool suits, with waisted jackets; Eleanor's is double-breasted. Sheila wears a coat with a velvet collar while their mother has a dark, warm-looking dress, belted at the waist, and a brimless, smart hat. Eleanor has a brooch on her lapel, a handbag over her shoulder and gloves. She's smiling, proud to be in her good clothes, her eyes are almost shut against the sunlight.

Eventually the dam got built, so too the power station. The construction workers left and Ballyshannon became once again a sleepy market town. Many businesses had started up during the boom years but were not sustainable any more. People wanted work done on credit, but as everyone knew everyone else and many were friends, they could be slow to pay their bills. At that time, many families emigrated, and in other cases, the men went away to find work, sending money back home.

My grandfather applied for a job in London with Telephone Cables, later moving to the BBC as a wiring technician. Granny Mac was left in charge of the shop and the business. But she was no businesswoman, and as Máire related it to me: 'She was clueless, and of course the staff fleeced her.' This would have been the mid-fifties. Máire had just finished her school exams, and decided to go to London too, finding work in the publications department of the BBC. On a return trip, Seamus realised the business was going downhill faster than ever and had to face the fact there was no future in it. He decided to sell up and move the family permanently to London. He was in his mid-forties by then and it can't have been an easy decision. For a pittance, they sold the three-storey, double-fronted shop as well as the cafe they owned next door and a large lockup garage in nearby Market House.

Eleanor was fourteen and coming up for her intermediate exam. Sheila senior's nun sister, Isabel, a charming lady who also liked the finer things in life, was headmistress of the Poor Clare school in Porthcawl, Wales, which took boarders as well as day girls. As Eleanor was considered quite clever, everyone thought she'd benefit greatly from going there. Sheila's spinster aunts, Janie and Celie, offered to pay the school fees.

So the family crossed the Irish Sea and lived in a rented flat in Brixton, near Seamus's work at Clapham. Máire went to work. Eleanor went to boarding school. Sheedy and Jim, being that bit younger, went to the local school where they were teased for their Irish accents.

When the money came through from the sale of the business and home in Ireland, Seamus found a house in Isleworth, West London. A two-up, two-down, with an extra little room tacked on the back over the kitchen and bathroom. A Victorian terrace with a lovely long garden trailing down to the small River Crane that ran into the Thames. Seamus soon grew heaps of vegetables and got himself a little boat to explore in.

It was a crowded house. At one time when Eleanor returned in school holidays, there were eleven people living there in a combination of bunks and in the attic. Máire said she felt sorry for her sister as she didn't have her own room.

It's quite a journey from Wales to London; you'd have to allow a full day. I find myself wondering now how she made that journey. By herself? By train? Bus? At each term break, and lugging a heavy suitcase, I guess.

Eleanor's schoolmates were mostly from well-off families who'd send them hampers and jam and spare money. Things were tighter in the McGonigle family, and she was always having to ask her father for little bits of money for toiletries and other necessities. No jam for Eleanor.

Again, the details are sparse. They had cold toast for breakfast at boarding school, I know that. Eleanor's drama and music ability was acknowledged; I know that too. She came away with a story of doing well at school, but part of me doubts, perhaps unfairly, how high the standard was.

She learnt the cello once Seamus had managed to get hold of one. Auntie Isabel, the headmistress, asked him to find one at the BBC. God knows what condition it was in! A surviving photograph shows Eleanor in white shirt and tie, one of a group of girls playing strings outside against a backdrop of a handsome building.

One year Eleanor was invited to holiday with a family in Switzerland, skiing, and that's where she met a young engineer just a few years her senior: Mike Haynes—my father.

As the time to leave school loomed, Eleanor planned a career as a speech and drama teacher and had a place in mind to carry on her study. They said she showed 'great promise' and she planned to go for auditions to the Central School in London and the Rose Bruford College in Sidcup.

But it never eventuated. One school holidays, according to Máire, Seamus had caught Eleanor and Mike kissing and cuddling at the front door after Mike had seen her home. Seamus wasn't having any of it. The upshot was that he refused to put his signature on the paper that would have given Eleanor a grant making it all possible to go to the drama school. She left home after a flaming row with her father. Whether she walked out, or was thrown out, is not clear. It was probably a bit of both. When she talked of it herself, she made it clear she wasn't going to be bossed about, either. It must have been very traumatic. She certainly saw it as a major event in her life; her big rebellion, taking a brave stand against her father.

She fled to Hastings, the seaside resort where Mike's parents lived. She found herself a bedsit and worked at Boots the Chemist. 'After all that education,' said Máire.

Eleanor and Mike were married the following year, in 1962. She was nineteen, he twenty-four. It was a civil ceremony. She wore a green suit. Máire, with her new husband, John, were the only family representatives on her side. Her father refused to be present while her mother and sister Sheila dared not go against his wishes and attend themselves. The family wasn't reconciled until I was born, a couple of years after Eleanor had dramatically left home.

She was married at nineteen and had her first baby— me—at twenty.

My mother loved to tell the stories of our births. When I was due, they lived in a flat in Kingston-upon-Thames in West London. They didn't qualify for a hospital bed, they always used to tell me, because they had an inside loo. Most births were at home then.

They'd ordered the 'layette'—everything you could conceivably need for a new baby, including pram and cot—but when Mum went into labour it hadn't arrived yet, because the baby was not yet due.

On a cold, cold February day in 1963 I appeared to be on my way—two weeks early. Dad went out into the snow to a public phone box to call the midwife. He'd read up on helping at a birth and was ready to go it alone should he need to. He knew what he needed: hot water, plenty, and a straw! I'm not precisely sure what the straw was for—but I imagine it was for sticking down my throat should it be blocked. I don't think I needed it!

He realised he didn't have the midwife's phone number

so had to ring directory enquiries. No pen either. So he wrote her number on the ice in the phone box windows.

All was well. I was born just a few hours later after a simple and, Mum insisted, painless labour. The young couple that were my parents made me a bed in the bottom drawer of a handsome chest of drawers. It was large, made of dark wood, with big handles that were round and smooth. My sister still has it.

I came across a letter Mum wrote me decades later, remembering the weeks around the time of my birth:

The snow was piled up on the pavements right up until after you were born. The roads were also bad, especially the side ones and the midwife had to come on her bicycle. I remember the first outing in the pram, to the laundrette at end of the road—very exciting! It started hailing so badly that the pram was filling up! I had to turn round and go back.

Kingston-upon-Thames was a quite a 'groovy' suburb in those days, in the sixties, and Mum and Dad planned to buy a place there. They had one lined up and were on the verge of buying it when one weekend they went for a drive and saw a house for sale in Seal, a village about an hour's drive from London, in Kent. They liked the country feel, the quietness. The village was surrounded by green fields, and had some picturesque old houses. They withdrew the offer on the place in London and plumped for village life instead; a two-bedroom house with a nice little garden which later sprouted a rabbit hutch and a swing as well as potatoes.

It was on a cul-de-sac and a good place for me to learn to ride a bike a few years later. I knew I had been born at a place that began with 'K' and as the only place I knew was the hills a few miles behind us, I told my other playmates I was born in Kemsing.

Dad told me that Mum learnt to drive in Seal, and it was he who taught her. She was very upset after one lesson, he said, when our cat came running to meet the car and ran under the wheels. I was only about one when we moved to Seal, so I was too young to remember that cat, or that incident.

Mum made friends, particularly with Pat and Owen, who already had two young daughters. They weren't quite neighbours but lived very close, just a minute or so's walk down the cul-de-sac and over the road.

Fiona came along two years after me. Another very short labour on a morning Mum was due to have friends round for coffee. She was a very easy baby as she slept such a lot. I asked once what sort of a baby I'd been, but didn't get much of a response, only to say Mum had to carry me around on her hip when serving coffee at coffee mornings. (Which didn't sound too much of a sacrifice!)

Dad had left school on the early side (much disrupted by his family's emigration to and return a year later from Australia, in his early teens) and did day-release study to qualify as a chartered engineer. He used to tell the tale of a job interview—maybe for a plum position—where he was asked what his wife wanted. 'At the moment my wife would like a washing machine,' the young Michael replied cheekily. The interview panel was not amused. He didn't get the job.

He got on, though. He travelled a fair bit—to Germany in particular, for months at a time. When I was three and Fiona one, we went to live in Malaysia for four months. I have very few memories of that time. An older American lady befriended me and I continued to write to her until my teens. She once took me out for lunch, which I found most exciting. I had a nasty fall and remember going to a black-skinned doctor who gave me a sweet and was very kind to me. Mum and Dad explored the nearby area, visiting temples and the like. But I don't have much of an idea of their lives then.

A few years later, this was the late sixties by now, Dad's job with an oil company took him to Australia, to Perth, where we ended up for about two years.

I remember packing up—all the boxes—and deciding which toys to take. Should I take the doll with the cut hair, or would other children laugh at it? I think I took it after all; it may even have gone to a 'dolls' hospital' and been given a new head of hair.

The single-storey houses in Australia seemed a little odd, but we soon got used to it. There were a few earthquakes around that time. Once, Mum was standing at the kitchen sink and felt a bit dizzy, then noticed the dishwater slopping around. She warned us to run out of the house if we felt a tremor, and warned us, too, about redback spiders.

We went to the beach on Christmas Day and I remember both the pavements and the sand being so hot you could hardly walk on them. Photos of the time show Fiona and me like little tanned elves, with gleaming white smiles.

I'd gone to a kindergarten for the first year we were there, as although I'd started school in England, the starting age was six in Perth. I had a pair of orange-and-white sandals with a big flower on the front. I had to take them off at kindergarten. I didn't like that at first. We didn't go barefoot much in England. Once I walked home on my own. Why did I do that? It was all right, I didn't get in trouble. Another time, I was helping push the pushchair with Fiona in it and we went over a snake.

I remember schools—I went to two there, in different

suburbs; being asked to spell 'biscuit'; that the girl next door had six toes; that a trick in another family was to turn your empty boiled-egg shell upside down and pretend you hadn't eaten it. There were biscuits with hard icing that if you licked and licked, made your tongue bleed.

I'd like to say that I remember Mum being happy—or unhappy—in these early years of my childhood, but of course, I can't. The most I can summon up is a general feeling of things being fine, a relatively easy life. Perhaps if I dig deep I can uncover a certain lightness in these times? Or am I on too uncertain ground? Mum and Dad must have gone out a bit in the evenings as I remember several babysitters. One, whose name I can't remember, used to wear a pale blue rollneck jumper with ski pants, probably very fashionable then! She broke the toy basket lid by pretending to fly off it during one of our games. Mum and Dad would have been still young. Mum would have been twenty-five when they left for Australia and Dad nearing thirty.

They went to drive-in movies and open-air concerts where you took a picnic basket and even wine. We went driving at the weekends and sought out ghost towns where we picked buckets of quartz that were later shipped back to England. We visited the old mining towns of Coolgardie and Kalgoorlie (I can still picture the life-size figures in the museum there) and saw whales being cut up in Albany. We counted squashed lizards on the roads and admired the brilliantly-coloured kangaroo-paw flowers. Dad liked Australia and wouldn't have minded staying longer, but Mum didn't want to stay. Some things were a bit rough compared to England. No genteel country pubs in buildings centuries old, for a start, but places that weren't welcoming in those times to women.

Towards the end, perhaps because the final leaving date kept moving, we spent several months in a serviced apartment complex, where Dad taught us to swim. It was here, I think, that I caught measles and had ghastly hallucinations and nightmares that I still remember, almost forty years later.

Then it was time to come back to England and to the house in Seal. Two years or so had passed. Before I left, I had had to stand on the toilet seat to pull the chain and flush the toilet. When we got back, I was tall enough to reach it myself.

The family expanded with the addition of a puppy, a bearded collie called Shannon, and a black rabbit called Blossom. We moved soon after to Ightham, another village a few miles away, to a larger, grander house with an acre of very private land. The house was built in 1913, and had handsome steps leading to a small porch. It had a large square hall with stairs leading off. And a sitting room to the left, dining room to the right, kitchen at the back, all with tall windows and, except for the small kitchen, good-sized rooms. The place had been a nursery but had got entirely overgrown again, turning back into the woods it was surrounded by. You could watch squirrels on the oak trees from the bedroom windows and hear the wood pigeons in the morning. The back gate of the garden led directly into the National Trust owned Oldbury Woods, where you could walk for hours among beech and oak trees and in the summer hear the rustle of an ants' nest among the leaf litter.

I was new girl at school again, but while I was considered fairly quiet, underneath it I wasn't shy, and wasn't daunted by making new friends again. I joined Brownies, played netball for the school and made camps with friends in the woods and at the recreation ground. In the woods we'd hunt for old bottles in the many leafy depressions. I soon had quite a collection.

Mum spent hours poring over interior design magazines, planning new colour schemes and curtains for the house. She organised alterations in the house, particularly a new kitchen extension, choosing units and doors and tiles for the floor.

Mum kept an organised, clean house. There was a fair bit of entertaining with company guests, drinks parties with canapés. She had a cleaning lady, Iris: a thin, wrinkly lady who smelt badly of cigarettes but was nice enough and good with the Brasso on the brass doorknobs.

I remember we had to tiptoe about Mum a bit. She was moody and 'don't upset your mother' was a frequent refrain. Manners were important; we could get sent to our rooms for a cheeky comment. And we learnt to help around the house. We did our own ironing from eleven or twelve and I was surprised to read quite a few diary entries from that age about dusting. 'Not until you tidy your room' is a phrase I remember from that era. Directed at both Fiona and me. It was a bore at the time, but nothing out of the ordinary.

By the time we moved to Ightham, Dad was into horses. He'd had a horse in Seal in Pat and Owen's field for a while, then in Ightham, they had a stable built. Back in England, Fiona and I started to learn, then became totally involved helping out at a little riding school called Mrs May's.

Mum had never been very adventurous physically. She liked the odd game of tennis, but (despite a couple of pictures I have of her in her childhood with bicycles) didn't like cycling and wasn't interested in trying horseriding.

We must have taken a lot of my mother's time. Ferrying us around to pony club things—although we were pretty independent from early on. Soon, all in the family bar Mum were fairly horse-mad. We didn't really question the fact that she didn't ride—horseriding's not everyone's cup of tea and we didn't see her as a very physical or outdoorsy person. She never seemed to feel left out, but took on a fringe interest in horses, gleaning a little about riding positions and pony behaviour from our chatter. On Saturday and Sunday my sister and I were out of the house by 7 am on our bikes to catch ponies, ride them miles in, tack them up, help with lessons and rides, clean saddles and bridles before riding them back to their fields. We'd arrive home, around 1 or 2 pm, with greasy hair and grimy clothes, we'd have a bath and wash our hair and, on a Sunday, Mum would cook a roast with all the trimmings: Yorkshire pudding, roast potatoes, gravy. Fiona and I would take it in turns to record the songs we liked on the Top 20 on BBC Radio 2, so each week one of us would be leaping up and down from the dining table to press the pause button on the tape recorder. This would have been the early to mid 1970s, the era of The Osmonds, David Essex (I really liked him!), Harry Nilsson's 'Without You', Paper Lace's sentimental, 'Billy, Don't be a Hero' as well as daft ones from the Wombles, or 'Knock Three Times on the Ceiling' and 'Chirpy, Chirpy Cheep Cheep'.

Mum liked Neil Diamond, I remember. As a young girl I used to listen to him singing The Hollies' song, 'He Ain't Heavy (He's my Brother)' and think it must be about someone pushing a friend or a brother in a wheelchair. It had that physical sense—I didn't hear it metaphorically. I once told Mum what I thought and got a dismissive response. I was quite taken aback when years later I heard the story of the song, inspired by a photo of a Vietnam War soldier who'd carried an injured Vietnamese man for miles and when asked if he'd carried him far, replied, 'He ain't heavy, he's my brother.' Checking on this story decades later, I realise there are many versions. It's a phrase with its own folklore, almost. The little girl I was then had got it right, yet there was never any encouragement to think like that. What I'm trying to explain, I suppose, is that Mum could be quite abrupt. She wasn't someone to talk things over with or explore ideas with. We didn't confide in her, or expect much affection. We always had what we needed for school, or Brownies: the right colour tights and socks, notes signed, whatever extras we had to have. But I don't remember her being there for us emotionally.

I don't knock that material provision, though—and really, when you think of it, it does translate from the emotional. When I had my first child, a friend of mine who was adopted at the age of two was quite shocked to see what care and labour went into even keeping a child clothed and fed from birth to age two. It made her realise both what her birth mother would have given her in those first two years, and also question how she could have finally given her up. I think my own mother was 'there' as much as she could be. And as a child, you don't know any differently. Maybe sometimes you thought someone else's mother was more fun, or looking back, with your own children, you think, I don't want to be like that. But really, your mother's your mother and that's that.

Once both my sister and I were at secondary school, Mum had the occasional job as a dentist's receptionist. She'd come back with stories of how he used hypnosis to anaesthetise his patients. For a good while she had a part-time job as a market researcher. They'd interview people and listen to focus groups on furniture polish, puddings and soft drinks. Occasionally, if they needed people in our age group we would participate, and on a few occasions in the holidays, we'd hang out there if Mum had to work. The business was owned by an amiable, outgoing lady who operated from a rather dishevelled house on an estate and would sometimes be seen in her bra as she ironed a shirt or went upstairs to change—a far cry from scenes in our home.

There was a constant stream of pets. Dad had horses after we got back from Australia. I'd had a hamster when I was very little, back in the house at Seal. I kept him by my bed and he'd whirr away on his wheel in the night. When we moved to Ightham, Blossom the rabbit escaped from his hutch! Little brown rabbits used to visit him in his cage, and one day, somehow, he got out. But he came back in the first winter for food. Mum and Dad looked after a friend's budgie and that also escaped into the wild when they were cleaning the cage. Shannon, too, now fully grown, came to a sad end—he ran off with an Alsatian who lived 100 yards away and they were both hit by a lorry. We all cried, and buried him at the top of the woodland garden, with a little wooden cross a girl had given me at school. Then Robbie, another bearded collie, came along. A big, hairy dog, who'd put his paws up on the hall table and bark at anyone coming up the drive and garden path to the front door—with his tail, out of sight, wagging madly.

Mum was not interested in horses or the outdoor life, but she was interested in other countries. We had French language students stay a couple of times. She went on a couple of holidays with Pat, the friend from Seal. One trip was to Sicily. They brought back little colourful toy carts with the horses dressed up in feathers. She took the travel seriously and read up about the history and culture of anywhere she went. She also went to Naples and Pompeii. She and Pat got a private tour of Pompeii through the 'back door'—it had been closed but a guide had taken an interest in them and shown them around. They'd had to climb over a fence to get in.

We went on holiday as a family too. Mum would research good places to go and she'd book a lovely thatched cottage in the country or in picturesque fishing villages in Cornwall or Dorset. Holidays meant a change in family routines and Dad, I seem to remember, would do more of the cooking than normal, especially when it came to making big cooked breakfasts which would keep us going throughout the day. There would be days on the beach, or visits to local castles, churches or other local attractions.

Mum was a good cook, but there were a few accidents that we all laughed about. The time she accidentally put salt instead of sugar in a pavlova (a recipe she'd brought back from Australia). And there was the time Robbie the dog ate the fruit cake.

When Dad was transferred to Trinidad for six months, Mum and Fiona visited during the Easter holidays, while I went on a French exchange program, staying with a French family. (Every year of my secondary school I spent the Easter holidays with this family, the Dubois, in Tours, while my correspondent, Emmanuelle, or Mannu, would come to us in the summer holidays.) They came back tanned, with stories of swimming all day and the steelpan bands by the pool.

We moved again another eight or so years after moving to Ightham, in the late seventies. The field where Dad kept his horse was sold and it was too difficult to find anywhere else to graze it. House details came in the post and they'd pore over them, even in bed, I seem to remember. We visited a few, then they bought a place on the Kent and Sussex border with 15 acres: 5 acres were woodland, plus three fields. It was a mile or so outside the village of Hawkhurst, in a dip in the land, at a bend of a tree-lined road. The house itself looked like a Scout hut, but it could be spruced up, altered and extended and it had the land they needed.

I was quite sad leaving Ightham. It was a lovely house, surrounded by woods. The walking and riding had been wonderful; as well as bridlepaths through the woods, there was Bedgebury Forest nearby, and, when you could go for a longer ride, cornfields to ride through. We'd had lots of happy Christmas days there. We put a tree in the hall, Mum hung Christmas cards on the back of the doors and cooked a turkey, sausages with bacon wrapped round, roast potatoes, vegetables. Mum always bought lots of stocking presents, which we'd find at the foot of the bed. We had been allowed to open them when it was light enough to see. There were card games with my grandparents before dinner—cribbage, or rummy—and walks in the woods afterwards. A few years, the walks were in the snow. A white Christmas. In the evening, when Nanny and

Granddad had gone home, we'd watch *The Great Escape*, or *The Sound of Music* on the television.

The new house was filthy. The previous owners had written all over the wall by the phone and Dad had to saw off the toilet seat before anyone would use it. I still preferred to nip up into the woods on that first evening. The cat, Manuel (who alone had survived the main road in Ightham), leapt up the chimney on arrival in the new house and refused to come down. The dog ran off with next door's and they reappeared at getting on for ten in the evening, looking like drowned rats.

Mum was always a good organiser. She set to cleaning up, unpacking and making the place habitable. The house was redecorated, a couple of walls knocked down, and very soon was a pleasant home to live in.

Manuel, our cat, grew muscly in his new environment. One morning I heard Mum screaming and shouting at him—he'd brought in a rabbit. An hour later there were more screams. Another rabbit.

The kitchen had an Aga: a cream-coloured range with two large hotplates with lids that you raised. Mum's first cooking experience on the Aga was a boiled egg. She waited for the water to boil but it never did. But when she took it off the hotplate after ten minutes it was hard.

She quickly learned its tricks, however, calculating when it would need more fuel and 'riddling' it in the morning to loosen and then remove the previous day's ashes. Christmas was the real test. She or Dad would get up in the early hours to put the turkey in the oven and it would slowly cook till the afternoon for a good spread.

Who is my mother at this time? A shadowy figure, dressed well, a tight face, often cross, rarely gentle, telling me to walk the dog or tidy my room. I peer into my memory, trying to find her. But I'm looking through the eyes of a five-year-old, then a ten-year-old and fifteen-year-old. The last slap, at fifteen years old. For a 'look like that' when I tell her the French exchange girls are frightened of her. Telling her exam results, and her response, 'That's not very good, is it?', when in fact I've come top of the class. When it comes to opinions, especially political, she stands behind my dad. Does she have any views of her own? They are a united front against my unformed, sensitive opinions.

One night, after I'd passed my driving test, I had a row over voting rights, being better than other people (mine were most egalitarian views) and went to spend the night with a friend. We must have had two cars then because I think I drove. Through the leafy dark lanes to a friend's house.

She softened later, perhaps she felt my sister and me moving out of her orbit and thought she needed to change her tune. Sometimes those explorations into a kinder attitude did not ring true.

She made some new friends. Not many friendships lasted. It wasn't so much a falling-out, but a petering out, leaving a gap to be filled by another name that would be heard a lot. Eccentricity was a magnet: when one friend started talking about her dog being poisoned by the neighbours, and milk being contaminated in the local shop ... Mum was fascinated.

In the early eighties, Dad was transferred to Egypt, to Cairo. I was in my last year of school, had my A levels at the end of the school year, and had applied to do medicine at Guy's Hospital. Fiona was doing her O levels and would be going to boarding school the next year. So Dad went first and Mum would join him later in the year. I was going to rent a flat with a schoolfriend and Fiona would go to a local mixed boarding school. She was happy with that option as the school had a reputation as being a fun place to be in the sixth form. In between, we'd visit during school holidays. Meanwhile, Mum organised a shipment to go to Cairo. It was all very exciting.

THREE

A SAD JOURNEY

I'm standing in Hounslow bus station. It's early morning.
It is grey. The wind is antisocial. The station is dirty and oily.
The buses are red and I'm not sure which stand the one
I need leaves from. There is litter flying around. The bus drivers
have dark faces. The shops are full of goods which will fall apart
soon after they're purchased. I've arrived in London for my
mother's funeral.

The plane journey was long, but uneventful. I had a window seat and looked out over the vastness of Australia: giant-sized ripples in red earth, enormous craters with black rock centres, surrounded by green, green dots, great salt lakes with creamy-coloured 'islands' and pale blue 'water'. Of course, I thought about my mother and the journey I was

making. I could hardly fathom that she really had gone and
that I was going to England for her funeral. Then I would
picture her sleepy figure curled up in bed as she'd been
found, her face looking tired. I thought about how I'd soon
be visiting her house, and how she would not be there. I
thought about how her body would have been moved, and
now dressed in her best, how I'd be seeing her body before
the funeral. All this, yet it still felt surreal. Then I'd look out
of the window again: now pink hills with a scattering of
green shadows, now the great sweeping lines of river beds.

On arrival in Heathrow, I made my way to Sheila's and
there, a little later, Dad met me and drove me back to
Hawkhurst, to the house he and Mum had lived in before
they had separated, but which he now shared with Anne.
The journey, which at best took one and a quarter hours,
seemed to take forever as the traffic was snarled up badly.

Fiona drove me to Mum's house. We took the only route
you can. Up to the main road. Past the old farm shop. Past
the baker which is popular and a good one, but you have
to make a precarious dash across the busy road to patronise
it. Past the pub, now a Chinese restaurant. Peter and I

treated Mum one year to a takeaway from there; it cost a fortune but she really enjoyed it and it was good to see her eat. Turn left by the hairdressers, through a little cluster of residential streets then plunging down the hill to Etchingham station. A twisting, dark road, with fields to the left, station on the flat a mile or so down. Over the crossing, the ancient church of Etchingham to the right. I went in there once with Mum, one of the few times she went out with me during those years of illness. The pew ends were special, she pointed out. I have an image of a little Harry there, dancing between spots of light coming through the windows, me shushing a few noises from him. Up through the village and then a straight stretch on to Burwash. (This was where, on one drive, one holiday, with Harry in the back seat, we'd been asked to stop by an unmarked police car, then witnessed a country police chase. We'd seen it all—the snaking of a car in front of the wanted one, the desperate climb by two well-attired men out of the car, over a large gate up a drive, and the police going after them and a few minutes later appearing with them in handcuffs.) Then the hill climbs and twists just a fraction, past Burwash church with its spire. Look out for the 30 miles an hour sign—that's where the drive is. Slow down, wait for a break in traffic and carefully, up the narrow drive, between two centuries-old buildings.

Fiona parked the car at the back by the garages. In other visits, Mum would be inside. She'd probably hear the car, know we were coming, maybe peep out of her sitting room window, upstairs, that looks out the back. When Harry was little he used to 'call' 'Grandma!' as we walked in the back door that she always left unlocked once she was up and about. Would she be in the kitchen? Upstairs? In later years, Felix and Harry argued about who'd 'do the calling' and took it in turns to 'call' then run in, through the dark, big room downstairs, with its handsome inglenook and green carpet. No boys this time.

Tears rolled down my face as I opened the little wrought-iron gate into her courtyard garden. Later I'd pick some rosemary and thyme. Fiona had the key to the back door. We walked in. Fiona had left the house as much as possible as she'd found it herself. There'd been a plate left after a snack in the sitting room downstairs which she'd washed up, and she'd had to look in drawers for documents, but she'd touched very little else. One of my first thoughts was how clean it was and how ironic that the alarm had been set off by Jackie coming to clean. There was nothing to do! Everything was neat, the little ornaments in their places as usual, the kitchen was tidy. The carpets were spotless. On the table in the kitchen was my Christmas present ready to wrap—a beautiful shiny cataplana, a Spanish copper cooking vessel, plus some gifts for the boys and some books that she must have just got from a mail order company that were apparently designated for various Christmas presents too.

Upstairs, the little sitting room smelt of lavender, from a lavender-filled pillow sitting on the sofa. The letter I'd posted only days before Mum's death was on the pine chest. She can only have received it a day, maybe two, before her last. She didn't keep letters and very soon they'd be put in the bin. A tapestry she was working on lay on the back of the sofa. She'd done the hard bit—the cream background—and there were only a few butterflies to finish. A notepad contained a letter started, but not finished, to me, next to it some newspaper cuttings it looked like she intended sending me. The bird feed holder was still outside her little window.

I walked into every room. In the bathroom in the washing basket was a small pile of clothes, just one day's wear by the look. In her bedroom, Fiona had folded the clothes she'd worn the day before she died: a smart pair of dark wool trousers and a pale lilac angora jumper. Some white slip-on sandals stood paired under a stool, the thick leather bumpy and lumpy, an unglamorous 'ghost' of her feet. There were a couple of novels by her bed—I don't remember their titles. Fiona had smoothed the duvet on her bed and plumped up the pillows.

I walked up the twisting steep stair to the top two rooms. The back one looked over the fields, the front onto the valley where Rudyard Kipling had walked when he lived at Bateman's, a few miles out of the village. Two single beds in each room were covered in yellow bedspreads with coordinating piping and an arrangement of cushions at the top and soft blue-and-white checked blankets at the bottom.

In a pine chest in one of the spare rooms was a bundle of papers about the planning of Peter's and my wedding. There were the seating plans, the menu, all the letters from friends and family responding to the invitation. There were also a few old toys. Fiona's pink fluffy teddy. Two Malaysian fabric dolls in traditional trouser suits. We'd had them as young girls. One was missing her little silk shoe, and only one had her baby on her back in a sling.

A couple of towelling dressing-gowns hung on the back of one door. One was a pink one of mine that a schoolfriend, Rachel, had made me when we still shared a flat together; another was a terracotta-coloured one of Dad's. Strange items, I had always thought, to have brought with her to this house. Maybe she liked the idea of being able to offer a surprise guest a dressing-gown, much like a hotel. On reflection, perhaps it was a little bit of Dad she liked to have, tucked away in a guest room, hanging silently, probably never used, on the back of the door.

I had decided early on that I would like to see Mum's body. It wasn't anything I'd ever given much thought to, although I was aware that some people thought it was a healthy thing to do, aiding the acceptance that someone really had died. While I was still in Australia, I rang Dad to tell him. Fiona had probably been driving up from Devon at the time. I knew that Mum would have to have an autopsy, and I didn't know what that would involve, but if it made any difference, I wanted it known that I'd like to see her one more time.

It turned out to be a bit of an issue as the delay between her dying and being buried was more than two weeks. Fiona had several 'condition of the body' discussions with the undertakers—including one bizarre conversation while she was driving back down to Devon one day. I'm not au fait with the details; I guess bodies these days are kept in chilled conditions in morgues, but for a number of reasons Mum's was expected to deteriorate more quickly. She was not in good health and was on a number of medications which would affect the flesh. 'Excuse the next bit. Not very nice but must be said,' Fiona had emailed, one morning. There were issues of bloating and blackening and tissue breakdown. Fiona did not wish to see Mum's body, so it was just a question of whether it was likely to be okay for me. She told the funeral director that during the year I'd done of medicine, I'd dissected human bodies, so I wasn't your average squeamish person. I told them both I obviously wasn't interested in seeing her if it would give me nightmares for the rest of my life.

In the end, the funeral director said they'd just have to see 'what she was like' when they 'got her'. In one of the numerous emails that passed between Fiona and me, I said that if it came to it, I'd just like to sit next to the coffin, lid sealed if necessary, if that was the closest I could get.

I arrived on a Sunday and on Monday we went to the house, then in the afternoon we were to see her body. It turned out that she was considered fit for viewing. Fiona and I trundled down the sunny high street, with its pollarded lime trees, past the post office, the little supermarket ... the places that had marked Mum's life in the last six years. The funeral directors' looked like an ordinary house. We knocked on the door and were greeted by a lady in a pale grey suit, fairly bright and breezy. We sat in a little waiting room, a bit like an ordinary sitting room. Pictures and ornaments on the mantelpiece, photographs on the walls. Catalogues of stones for tombs and order of service styles were the only giveaway.

A pleasant man led us down the drive to what seemed a bit like a garage set up at the back. We walked into another little waiting room and in the room next door was Mum.

Fiona had decided at the last minute that she would see Mum. Just in case she regretted not getting the chance. We had been quite matter-of-fact, but by now the tears were beginning to roll. Sheila had given me a rosary to place with Mum. It was their mother's, our Granny Mac's. I showed the funeral director and he said he'd put it on for me. He went into the room first and when he came out I asked him what we'd see. 'She's in there, facing away from the door, in her coffin. It's just a small room, you can stay as long as you like,' he said. We entered. Immediately I noticed Mum's hands, lying on top of her body. They were slightly swollen, just lifting them out of their normal bony look, and the moons of her nails were black. I knew the body had been through a lot since her death. The rosary was carefully and intricately placed around her hands. We walked the side of the shiny yellowy wooden coffin and saw her face. 'She looks just like she's asleep, doesn't she?' said the funeral director. Fiona and I looked at each other but didn't say anything.

After a few moments he left us alone together. 'God, it doesn't look anything like her!' we burst out. The jaw line was so puffy it changed the shape of her face entirely. Maybe it was the fact she was lying down, that in life our skin and flesh moves with gravity. If I'd seen a photograph of her like this I would not have recognised her. Her eyes were shut and her face was obviously covered with make-up. We were half expecting cut-marks on her skull from the autopsy, but there was no sign of it. Apart from her hands, the rest was covered up with the jacket and skirt Fiona had chosen. They were smart, but being meant for living people, they looked odd and out of place—not shabby, but somehow not as smart as usual. Or maybe it's merely the incongruity of seeing someone dressed up to their nines lying down in a coffin. How much nicer and more peaceful it would have been to see her as she'd died, curled up asleep under the covers, in, yes, I'd had to know, a large T-shirt-like nightie.

I was surprised how weighty she looked in the coffin. She was a thin lady; too thin. But you couldn't deny the presence and substance of her body filling that box.

Fiona didn't stay long. 'See you back at the house.'

I was glad to have some time with Mum alone. I walked around the coffin, peering at her face from different angles, trying to catch a view that did look like her. Her brow, I decided, with its thin skin and slight boniness just above her eyebrows. That was the same. Later, looking through pictures of her at different times—photos from ten, twenty, thirty years ago—I noticed that although many aspects of her face changed: lines, swelling, expressions evolving from a sort of cockiness to a brave face, one that sometimes seemed to be looking out of her own confined world, that little part of her forehead was the same.

I tested her hand. It was freezing cold.

Her hair. That was the same. She never had great hair. Not enough of it and not much oomph. Visits to the hairdresser—sometimes for colouring, sometimes for a blow-dry—were a regular event. While her sisters had gone grey gracefully, she'd hung on to more youthful hues. She already looked ten years her senior; I guess with grey hair she'd have looked even more beyond her sixty years.

I'd come bearing gifts to place with Mum. Máire and Sheila had both given me sealed crisp white envelopes, I had paintings from Harry and Felix, notes from my nieces, Hope and Harriet. From me—the piece of white bougainvillea from our garden in Sydney that had been blooming the morning I heard the news of her death, and a postcard I'd sent her which arrived too late. I placed the items one by one around her legs and feet. I was glad to be able to do it.

Her hair made me smile that day, lying in her coffin, her troubled body having gone through God knows what journeys—from the sunny plush bedroom, in an ambulance to the morgue. Out for an autopsy and back up here for preparation and dressing. A final, strange attention. Her hair, cut in a sort of short bob, had a little frizz to it that day.

I touched it with my forefinger. It was soft, almost baby-like. I would have liked to kiss her, but it seemed unwise—I'd only meet make-up and I didn't really know what was going on underneath—so I kissed her frizzy, soft hair and said Goodbye.

I walked back up the high street feeling lighter in my step and calmer. Fiona was back at the house. We sat and talked. 'I feel better for seeing her,' I told Fiona.

Fiona recoiled, 'Oh no … I didn't like it.' Wrinkling her nose, she said, 'Did you see her legs!' I did see her legs. They were jet-black in the opaque tights Fiona had selected. 'They were black!' Fiona continued.

'They were her tights,' I reminded her, and the tension broke with a howl of laughter. I reached for a fragile Belleek snowman and it made a delicate tinkling sound that made me smile. I put it aside to keep.

We decided to go the Bell Inn for some lunch. 'I'd better wash my hands,' I said, heading for the downstairs loo.

'Did you touch her?' Fiona said, amazed. 'Oh, I couldn't have done that!'

Seeing Mum's body was another hurdle crossed and somehow, somewhere, we found things to laugh about. We'd said before what a waste of good wood the coffin was. Fiona had joked about recycling the wood for a coffee table. We didn't feel the same now, but we could still laugh about it. I had a glass of wine with my lunch. Fiona had decided to give up alcohol. She said she reacted badly to it, even if she only had a little. So she stuck to water or juice. I decided to have a second glass. What the hell! I wasn't driving and it wasn't every day you viewed the body of your dead mother.

We went back to the house and Fiona sprung on me that she wanted to start dividing Mum's things. We had planned to do it after the funeral. But although Fiona had been keen to leave the house as it was, for me to see, she was now restless to at least begin the task of clearing it and emptying it—which, we had agreed, would start with each of us choosing items we wanted. Mum had envisaged Sheila and Máire taking a few things, but it was to Fiona and me that she left her house stuffed with its furniture and beautiful things. 'We'll just start with the books,' Fiona said.

I felt hamstrung. I didn't mind too much in principle. But I'd promised myself a little ritual—and had told Fiona about it. I wanted to open a bottle of Mum's champagne and raise a glass to her, say thank you and mark the transition between Cygnet Cottage being her home and it being a house that was being shed of its ownership. I guess there was also a small symbol of forgiveness in the gesture, forgiveness for her wrecking her health and her life. I had been angry at times with her for all sorts of reasons: being weak, I guess; being selfish; being difficult. I wanted to formally put that all behind me right there, in the home she had created. And it couldn't be with a cup of tea.

So having set that in my mind, I felt compelled still to do it before starting to dismantle Mum's home. I'd put a bottle from the cellar in the almost empty fridge—it shared the space with a carton of milk we bought with money from Mum's purse—so I popped it, polished a glass from the cabinet in the large sitting room, poured myself a glass and said, 'Thank you, Mum.'

Then, with wine and champagne flowing in my bloodstream along with jet lag and grief, we set about choosing books. Taking it in turns, one by one. There were some I thought Fiona should have. The Stephanie Alexander *Cook's Companion* that I'd given Mum. I already had a copy. It weighed a ton and had cost $50 to post. The cost did not elude Mum. While it's not an approach she took herself, part of her admired the fact that I would just buy what I wanted for people regardless (to an extent) of weight and put up with mailing costs.

I was keen on the books on English churches; Fiona took some reference books. I chose a poetry book, Fiona another. Our piles grew. Some of the books—like one on the history of costume—I could remember being around as long as myself. I remember looking at the pictures as a child. The strange turn of a foot in a drawing of someone from the sixties wearing a poncho; the cleavage of a medieval lady.

'I was just about to ask Mum to return this one,' I said, fingering *The Year 1000*.

'That doesn't count as a choice, then,' Fiona said.

There were some I thought Peter would like. Fiona took the odd one for a friend, or ones she knew Hope or Harriet would find useful.

Mine were mostly reference books—the *Oxford Biographical Encyclopaedia*, the *Cambridge Guide to Literature in English*—history, poetry and a few cookery ones. Nigella Lawson's *How to Eat*. The title intrigued and irritated at the same time. I'd never have parted with money for it, but it was a nicely produced volume. I didn't take many novels. We had different tastes. Mum's was mainly lighter (trashier, I secretly thought), although we had a little crossover and she'd lent me a couple that I loved. She introduced me to Penelope Fitzgerald (*The Blue Flower* and *The Bookshop*) and had lent me a book by Beryl Bainbridge about the *Titanic* which was compelling and had inspired me to search the internet for information on the passengers. I'd found many names reflected in the story, and had even delved into court transcripts.

On the top floor was a pine bookshelf that must have been one of the first pieces of furniture that Mum and Dad bought together. I could remember it being in various houses for as long as I took notice of that sort of thing. It was plain but of good quality. We were going through every shelf methodically, picking out volumes. I took a small red book and opened it. 'Eleanore McGonigle, Form V' was written on the inside front cover, in Mum's writing. We looked at it incredulously. Eleanore. What was with the extra 'e'? Was she really Eleanore, not Eleanor? Another 'e' might not seem much, but it seemed a lot at that moment. Had she changed her name? Dropped the 'e' or added it? Then we came across a stash of certificates. Piano, speech and drama ... There was the extra 'e' again. On several certificates and then not. Somehow it seemed quite shocking.

Later, we asked Sheila and Máire about the extra 'e' and they said affectionately, 'Oh ... that was her "Eleanore" phase.' We asked what they meant. 'She thought it was posh, so changed the way she spelt her name for a while,' they explained simply. She must have made quite a thing about it because of all the certificates, and we also found prayer cards from her friends, many to 'Eleanore'. Then I guess, for some reason known only to her, she dropped the pretension.

Although Dad had said that generally speaking he didn't want anything from the house, there were a couple of things he was keen to reclaim. One was a set of worry beads from their time in Egypt, another a gold puzzle ring. The worry beads were not with Mum's jewellery, nor on display anywhere.

As we were going through the books, I sat on the floor and peered up at the bookshelves, feeling slightly the worse for wear with the champagne. What was that on the top? It was a fawn-coloured ceramic jelly mould. Fiona took it down and there inside were the worry beads. Black with white specks and a tassel.

I didn't have anything suitable to use as a handbag at the funeral. The only thing I'd brought with me was more like a school satchel. Mum had heaps of bags; I thought I'd be able to select something of hers. Before going to the funeral directors', I looked through her collection. I couldn't have used her 'current' one—it was too personal, too full, and too big anyway. Another regular one she used was, with its red and pink flowers, too colourful. Then there were ones she'd hoarded over the years—navy, white, black ones, with trims, zips, poppers ... But most were too curly with age or too entrenched in another fashion era. I settled for an envelope-sized evening bag with dull black beads twisted over stiff black silk. It had a clean hanky inside with an embroidered corner. Perfect.

The night before Mum's funeral I felt extraordinarily tired. Jet lag was getting the better of me, so, hardly being able to keep my eyes open, I went to bed at 8 pm. I dreamt of being broken in to and fighting off the intruders, feeling doubly victimised as, and I told them so, my mother had just died. I woke at 11 pm and could not get back to sleep.

Strangely, in the morning, despite having slept only three hours, I didn't feel particularly tired. Body chemicals do wondrous things at times like this, smoothing out the emotions and feelings.

Having decided I wanted to speak at Mum's funeral, my main concern was getting through my 'tribute' without breaking down. I felt strongly that someone who loved her should talk for her—not just the rector, who, although he may have had an acquainterly fondness for her, would be very much the professional on board. I also wanted to acknowledge the fact that she'd been difficult at times. There would be several people in the congregation whom she'd fallen out with and had had nothing more to do with—and some whom she'd cut contact with, even though there'd been no quarrel. I was very glad they could be there. It did help. How sad it would be to go to a funeral of someone you loved and find few people attending.

Kelvin, Fiona's ex-husband, arrived at my dad's house. Four of his girls were with him: my nieces, Hope and Harriet, and his older girls, Florence and Sophie who, with their sister, Celia, had been bridesmaids for Peter and me more than ten years ago. Florence had shivered outside the church in her Laura Ashley needlecord flowery dress that Mum had chosen for them all. It had turned out to be the coldest day of the year, with frost on the grass and crumbling lichen-covered gravestones. Mum still had a picture of Florence by her piano. She had been fond of them and sorry to lose contact once Fiona and Kelvin split up. Apparently on hearing the news of Mum's death, the girls had said they'd like to come to her funeral. Very, very sweet of a couple of teenagers. I was very touched that Kelvin and those 'big' girls—as Hope and Harriet called their half-sisters—could come. Kelvin was wearing a thin plain black tie. It looked so miserable. It was a bit of a shock too, when Dad appeared wearing a similar version.

I couldn't help thinking of the gathering of the same people for our wedding, almost eleven years before. In this house. In this room. The same feeling of gathering for something special. Still going to a church—different one—but for such different reasons. Our wedding was a feat of organisation for my mother. She loved it. Choosing flowers for the pews, for me. How the cake should be decorated—who to make it—how many tiers. Where we'd have the reception (Did we want a disco? No, we'd do without); what we would eat, what wines we'd drink. We let her get on with it … she was happy. We were happy. She even tracked down the lines Peter remembered from his schoolboy renditions of 'He Who Would Valiant Be'. We chose hymns based on their singability. I'd gone to so many weddings and christenings and the like where people had chosen hymns with notes that a lay congregation—as opposed to a choir—just could not reach. By no means are all songs good when sung by both male and female singers. So 'He Who Would Valiant Be' was one choice and 'All Things Bright and Beautiful' another. But my hymn book didn't have the line that Peter remembered so well, and me too: 'Hobgoblin nor foul fiend/ Can daunt his spirit.' It was a watered-down version instead that we found. But Mum set to. She looked in every hymn book she came across and eventually found the words in a Scottish hymn book. New Zealand, where Peter grew up, has a strong Scottish ancestry and it seems they took their version of the hymn with them.

Last time I was pinning my hair up, touching up my

lipstick, checking the bridesmaids knew what they had to do. Hope wasn't around then but Harriet was—a bald-headed, smiling one-year-old in a red dress with a blue collar. She'd sat in a highchair eating toast. Getting ready for a wedding, spirits were high and happy. This time, in the hours before Mum's funeral, I didn't feel like chatting. I didn't want to explore feelings or exchange memories or even condolences just yet.

Fiona and I drove to the church in plenty of time. Fiona had the service orders. I had my tribute tucked in the bag and a second copy to give the rector as he'd recommended—so that he could continue reading what I wanted to say, just in case I couldn't go on.

At first I sat at the front of the church. I thought I needed to stay 'collected'. Fiona stood at the back of the church, near the heavy wooden doors. A few people I didn't recognise were already in the pews. I guess they were from the village, or maybe the history class Mum had been going to for some time. I heard a bit of a squeal from the back. It was Pat, her long-time friend from Seal that she'd holidayed with in younger days. I walked towards the entrance. She was crying. 'I did call her,' she said. 'I did try and keep in touch.'

I have no idea of funeral etiquette. Fiona seemed to like standing near the entrance, so I ended up there too, meeting and greeting. Our three tall cousins, Máire's sons, walked in looking very dashing in incredibly stylish, tasteful suits. They each kissed our cheeks. Some people signed a book which was lying on a table. 'They'll only get an invitation to my next service,' joked the rector later.

Hope decided she wanted to see the hole that was already dug for Mum's coffin. She went off almost cheerfully but came back aghast and in tears. It was so deep, cutting in to the dark earth. Something so tangible, you couldn't escape the reality of it.

Eventually we all sat down. Fiona, Dad and I, the immediate family, were at the front. All three of Mum's siblings were there: Máire, Sheila, and Jim, whom I hadn't seen for years, partly because Mum hadn't been talking to him.

'Here comes the music,' I smiled to Fiona. I thought it would sound terribly sentimental and maybe even over-the-top but in fact it was just lovely. The bearers walked in with Mum's coffin on their shoulders. They were dressed in dark suits with long tails. I didn't know any of them. The coffin looked beautiful. Mum would have approved. It had a single arrangement covering the entire top. Mostly white, lots of lilies, and a little splash of red. It was beautiful and simple. The music fluttered in the church and it was comforting to think that Mum had wanted this music to be playing. 'Time to Say Goodbye'. It was just that, but the words seemed to ease us into it, sad but hopeful because of its sheer beauty.

The coffin sat at the front of the church well within my view. I felt its presence very strongly and could hardly keep my eyes from it. I think the fact that I'd seen my mother in it—that I knew what was inside—brought it home unlike other times when all I saw was coffin.

I liked the service. There was something 'nice' about it being taken away just a little from yourself. Both comforting and cultivated, civil. Those closest, and those who would miss Mum in a personal way, would grieve in their own fashion. But the service seemed to say, 'We've done this before. We'll be doing it again. This is what we do.'

When the time came, I stood up, behind the eagle on the pulpit and spoke:

My mother's death is terribly sad, but it is not tragic. She had made herself a new life here in Burwash, forged new friendships and found a new rhythm in village life. Her hold on life was a fragile thread these past six years but she held on to that thread with tenacity.

She was at her best with a bee in her bonnet about one project or another—whether it was to start a history class in the village, or take it upon herself to find a new home for a friend's dog. She could be charming, she had a ready sense of humour ... she was certainly never bland and the fact she defied doctors for so long shows what a lot of pluck she had.

She was not always an easy person, and some people here had a difficult relationship with her at times: she was only human. She was capable of enormous strength and courage—she was rarely sentimental about her illness and often optimistic. I sometimes wonder if she would have been happier with a career. She had planned at one point to be a drama teacher, she would have made a good interior designer. But in the end, whether she was a wife, sister, mother, grandmother, friend or neighbour, we loved her for being Eleanor Haynes and we will miss her.

I'm glad I spoke for Mum. I wanted to speak out, acknowledge my and others' love for her despite everything. To say that she was a friend, neighbour, wife, sister, mother and grandmother and that we'd miss her. She'd failed herself in some ways, but been so brave in others. I'd got through it, catching my breath just the once. I sat down, reaching into Mum's black clutch bag for a handkerchief. It made me smile—it smelt of moth balls.

Later in the service the rector said how God said 'blossom where you are planted.' That was just what Eleanor did do, he observed—in Burwash, that is. That was the funny thing. Her immediate family felt she hadn't blossomed throughout her life but it was true that despite it being really hard for her when Dad left her—and God, when I think of it, even though I don't blame him, it must have been so hard, fifty-odd years old, all your feelings of status wrapped up in your marriage, such vulnerable pride battered and bruised—despite almost killing herself, she made a place for herself in a new community. Maybe she'd been taken outside herself a little more, too. The rector told me he had seen her just days before she died and ticked her off for doing so much for everyone.

In that cool, stone church, we sang 'Jerusalem': 'And did those feet in ancient times/Walk upon England's mountains green?…' I'd always found the words faintly ridiculous but beautiful. Mum had a strange relationship with greenery and the countryside. She seemed to like living in the country and to be surrounded by trees and fields, but I never felt her love for it went very deep. She enjoyed the trappings—green wellingtons, antique mud-scrapers by the back door, pine cones in a trug in the sitting room—and no doubt, the space and peace afforded by being out of town. I don't know her views on hymns—it's not something you necessarily talk about much!—but I hoped she'd have liked the imagery. 'Bring me my arrows of des-ire ... Bring me my char-i-ot of fire ...'

We ended the service with 'Morning has Broken'. I wanted to finish on an up note—a feeling of completing the circle, that what we'd been experiencing was part of the cycle of life, not an end in itself. And for all of us, whether we grieved deeply, or shed a few tears that were easily brushed away, we'd be experiencing a new morning breaking again and again.

We followed the coffin out, Fiona, Dad and I who were close behind. I'd chosen some Celtic music for that section. A gentle rendition of 'Sally Gardens' with guitar and Irish bouzuki. It was a small nod to Mum's Irishness as well as a subtle acknowledgement of the Irish relatives. There had been some talk, late in the piece, that she'd wanted Daniel O'Donnell singing 'Danny Boy', but I couldn't quite see it—and didn't want to hear it. This was more fitting, I felt. (The funeral director also asked if he could record it, he'd liked it so much.)

We walked out into the lovely little churchyard, higgledy-piggledy tombstones, old and new among the mowed grass, under yew trees and the rolling green hills stretching out beyond the village. The rector, in his robes, spoke again and the coffin was lowered into the ground. As the eldest child,

I was first offered earth to drop into the hole. I hadn't expected it, but stepped into the role easily, sprinkling a handful of dirt onto my mother's coffin. Fiona next. Dad was offered, but declined.

As we left the graveside, the funeral director greeted me. 'What was it like seeing your mother yesterday?' he asked.

I was slightly taken aback, having just watched her coffin going into the earth. 'I was glad to see her,' I replied. 'I felt better afterwards.'

'We were very pleased how she turned out,' he confessed in a matter-of-fact tone. 'She was in a bit of a state when we got her.'

Walking back to the reception at the Crown Inn, a neighbour of Mum's congratulated me on my tribute. 'I thought you wrapped up your mother very well,' he said, nodding.

'We had a couple of fallings-out with her,' his wife confessed.

'Did you?' I said. I'd not heard of these ones.

'Usually about our cat.'

After the reception—which was a polite collection of relatives, some old but often estranged friends, and some new ones—Fiona and I went out to dinner. Dad had insisted. He and Anne were going out to see a film. He hadn't wanted to be at the reception; she hadn't wanted to be part of a debriefing of Mum's funeral. Dad didn't like the thought of Fiona and me at the house alone, so we agreed. We went to Sanky's, a downstairs busy bistro in Tunbridge Wells. I'd been there quite a bit with Mum, and also for a fabulous meal or two with Peter. We spent the last of Mum's cash from her purse on our meal, but barely touched our dishes. I had mussels—moules marinières. Neither of us felt like wine. The funeral was a milestone and it had gone well, but we felt sad and tired.

Once the funeral was over, we continued sorting through the house. I mentioned I'd like the painting of the boys on the beach. I wanted to carry it back to Australia with me. It took on a particular significance. She had bought it with money she was given when an aunt had died. I wanted it to hang in my house as soon as possible as a reminder of Mum and her home. Dad offered to wrap it carefully for me for the journey. We agreed that it should be allowed as hand luggage.

On the top of a basket of magazines was a tarot card reading that Mum had written out, filling an A4 sheet of lined paper. The tarot cards were a bit of a secret in some ways. She'd wanted a set, and when asked what she wanted for her birthday the year I was in England, she'd said she'd like some tarot cards. Sheila and I had gone to Rye and I'd found a handsome set in one of the shops. I'd also bought her a couple of books on the subject: one that seemed very authoritative, and another that was more of a gift book with a chatty, entertaining overview. She hadn't wanted Máire to know because she thought she'd say how silly it was, so we weren't allowed to mention it to her, even though it didn't seem such a big deal to us. Mum must have come across or seen an ad for a teacher, because she started having lessons. Individual ones. She found it very interesting, and her teacher said she had flair. She did a few readings for those in the know, including, occasionally, a friend.

We studied her last reading with interest. The details elude me, writing this now, and Fiona had got rid of it fairly soon as she didn't want to get hooked on 'reading' too much into it. But the death card had come up for October or November. Death, with its skeleton, doesn't necessarily mean that literally in tarot. It's usually more of a new start, which we interpreted as a new start for us, a new era of our lives without our mother.

Mum did not generally keep letters. She did not keep mine, which was a shame as I'd have liked to have them back as a sort of diary. When she moved in on her own I used to write postcards to her two or three times a week. The only ones remaining were a black-and-white postcard, with bathing beauties in wooden swimsuits. I'd circled the caption and added a few exclamation marks. My letter that I'd posted just a few days before her death was on the floor of the upstairs sitting room.

There were only half a dozen or so other letters in the house in various drawers. I assume they held particular significance for her. Among them, one from Elizabeth, her schoolfriend who was Fiona's godmother. We'd always been told that she had died in the bath in hospital. Elizabeth's letter alluded to depression and illness.

Then there was one from Elizabeth's sister, in steady, neat writing, sent to Mum when we lived in Australia for a couple of years in the late sixties, when my sister and I were little girls, telling her of the sad news of Elizabeth's death.

She'd kept a letter from my grandfather on my father's side, signed 'Dad' and written entirely on the left-hand side of some thin notepaper, his shaky words floating eerily above the lines. She'd cut off Nanny and Granddad, as I called them, soon after Dad left her, not returned phone calls ... not sent Christmas cards. Granddad's letter told her that they'd not had a good year, with another stroke. I see her keeping it as a sign that they still meant something to her, even though she couldn't bring herself to keep in touch. After all, she was only a young thing when she first met them and had gone to live near them in Hastings. They were a steady presence throughout her adult life and had visited her and Dad in Cairo and later in Houston. They were kind people who cared, whether or not she returned it, but perhaps she did.

She had an old folded letter with, while not a Penny Black, another old stamp. In sepia ink, the letter told of the death of a sister from childbirth. I don't think it was a family letter, but one she must have come by in an antique shop, perhaps.

Mum had kept just one letter from my father, written soon after she'd moved out of the house at Hawkhurst. Perhaps I should not have read it, but I did. I felt a strong desire to uncarth whatever clues I could that might help me understand my mother. The letter told her, as if out of duty, what alterations Dad was making to the house to accommodate Anne's ageing parents. While on one hand it seems an unlikely letter to keep, on the other, I understand that strong curiosity about and identity with a place where you lived for twenty years. There was also a letter from a friend I'd never heard of who appeared to be living abroad, a recent friend I'd say, full of news of extravagant outings and name-dropping that would have appealed to Mum.

If my mother didn't keep letters, she made up for it by keeping clothes. She had five wardrobes of clothes plus a large cupboard filled with T-shirts, jumpers, cardigans, underwear and night gear: one in her bedroom, a lovely old pine one on the landing, plus a rail she had built for her coats, one on the landing upstairs and one in each of the spare bedrooms upstairs. There were clothes we were familiar with seeing her in recently: cosy, warm, luxurious jumpers, straight skirts, smart trousers, jeans that never looked quite right—as if she couldn't quite pull off her efforts at looking casual. Tailored clothes: Jaeger suits in smooth fabrics, with expensive buttons, little fitted jackets, pleated skirts. Her party clothes were the saddest: a black lace and velvet off-the-shoulder number, flounces of chiffon, raw shot-silk long skirts, heavily embroidered shirts. A whole wardrobe of clothes to wear to the opera, to company functions at ritzy hotels, to special invitations to the theatre, with lipstick and perfume. When was the last time she'd worn these? I wondered.

Mum's underwear was a revelation. She liked her designer labels on top but settled, it seemed, for Tesco knickers! A couple of pairs of thick walking socks caught my attention. She didn't go hiking. What did she need those for? For keeping out the cold, I later figured. She had bad circulation and suffered with the cold. Perhaps she wore them in bed.

I put aside a few jumpers I thought I might wear. I knew Mum would want us to use whatever we could. I picked the hiking socks and a couple of plain cotton shirts, a suede skirt and a black-and-white long kilt which, to be honest, I doubted I'd ever fit, but took anyway.

Among the linen in her bedroom, Fiona found a small plastic box. False teeth! She'd had several out at the front at a very young age, before she was married even. It wasn't something she would ever, ever have talked about, but I have a vague memory of seeing them, just the once, when I was about five, in the bathroom in our house in Seal. Maybe I said something and she made sure they were never seen. I'd certainly never set eyes on them ever again until now.

Mum had kept summer dresses from years back. Strappy, printed dresses I remember her wearing in Egypt. Ones I've seen her in in photographs. I felt a touch of betrayal in not taking these items, in not gathering up these particular memories.

She must have had thirty belts—thin, thick, outrageous, classic—hanging over a wire on the back of the bedroom wardrobe. Lots of shoes. Her feet were just half a size bigger than mine and I had imagined I might keep a few pairs but those with her imprint, I didn't really want, and many, though good quality and simple, were just not my style. I have her ankle boots with a bit of a heel and a couple of lace holes. They are hardly worn. They'll last me a good few years as although I'm hard on shoes, as I walk such a lot, these will be more 'special occasion'; I'm not one for even a small heel.

Mum must have had at least a dozen coats. Maybe more. All of them good quality ones too. It seemed such a waste. I was going to take any item of clothing I thought I might wear. Fiona said she didn't want anything, but she tried on a coat, a straight black one, and took that. I tried on a Hobbs one that she'd bought in Tunbridge Wells when I'd been with her. She'd baulked at the price then decided to get it anyway. Who did she have to ask? What was she saving money for? It was belted and had a rich, heavy swing to the skirt, with big folded-back cuffs. I tried it on. It felt fantastic, sitting squarely on my shoulders. She still had the price tag in the pocket.

'I've been thinking about it,' I announced to my sister. 'Mum's colours. Red and duck-egg blue.'

I'm not sure my statement got much reaction, but to me the colours said something about our mother. She liked vivid red and with, originally, at least, her dark hair, it suited her. Bright, vivacious. Harsh, angry. There was her softer side too.

Vulnerable, sensitive. Sad, lonely. I don't remember her wearing much of it in her younger days, but definitely a colour she became drawn to once she was ill was a soft, gentle, pale blue. She had a pale blue pashmina and a cosy twosome of cardigan and jumper. Jaeger. Fine angora and wool. A pale blue supersoft cashmere cardigan with pockets.

When she went out in later years, she usually donned the red. I remember her taking Sheila, Máire and John and me to the Powdermill, the year I took one-year-old Harry back to the UK, the first time I'd seen her since her collapse and spell in hospital. It was a beautiful country restaurant with a spacious, sunny dining room. Starched tablecloths, stunning flower arrangements, glittering glassware and cutlery. It wasn't a place for a baby, so Dad had looked after Harry for me. Mum had made herself up. Red lipstick. Powder. Walking stick and red suit. She looked quite good, considering, and was lively.

The blue seemed to me like a recognition that she needed something gentler to frame her frailty. Maybe the blue was the home colour, for the private life—be gentle on me; while the red helped her summon up her public face.

Something we shared out piece by piece was Mum's jewellery. Her collection wasn't extravagant, but she had a few pieces I admired and several she was proud enough of to have got valued. Some reached back into fresher, more innocent times: the tiny-faced gold watch with delicate bracelet that was a present for her eighteenth birthday. Others witnessed the years in Egypt: a clunky ring with a large lapis lazuli stone, a chunky Bedouin silver bracelet.

Fiona and I sat on one of the single beds in the spare room where we were sleeping at Dad and Anne's. The jewellery was in a leather jewellery roll with a slim buckled strap and several Chinese soft-zipped purses and bags. When we were going through the house, Sheila had reminded us to look in pockets—dressing-gowns, cardigans, coats. 'She used to hide bits of jewellery in them, she was always saying.' We looked in all the pockets but only found tissues. Lots of them.

We picked our choices one by one, much as we had meticulously shared out the contents of the large tins of Quality Street sweets that her father, Grandpa Mac, used to give us for Christmas. I still remember the mound of shining wrappers—purple, silver, green, red—and the exactitude of the division. The strawberry creams and flat, round toffees in a golden yellow wrapper were always left till last.

I chose some very plain gold earrings, simple pearl-sized studs, her watch, a Chinese medallion she used to wear on top of a jumper. The cameo pieces I'd always liked: a brooch and a ring. For some strange reason they remind me of our Ightham house in its acre of woodland. One evening, when my parents were out I'd gone into their bedroom and used some of Mum's nail varnish remover. Horror of horrors: I spilt some on the chest of drawers—a smooth finished reproduction piece with heavy rings for handles. It left pale puddle-shaped marks on the dark wood. Mum and Dad were back sooner than expected and they'd seen me in the bedroom, as they walked from the slab of concrete that marked where a garage might go at the top of the drive, past where lilies-of-the-valley grew on a short path to the house. I was surprised there was no fury directed my way. Perhaps they'd had a good time out and what might have caused a scene some other time was forgotten.

I put the cameo ring on that evening. It was a lot bigger than the style I usually wore.

'Don't you think it might upset Dad?' Fiona was concerned.

'Well, we can't pretend she's not dead, can we?' was my answer. It was bad enough not to be able to talk freely about her in the house. I felt proud to wear her ring as an acknowledgement and a sign that she'd left us and we were thinking of her.

Fiona thought we should also have a 'convert' pile. Showy

pieces that we knew we'd never wear but might be quite valuable. She'd do a 'diamond run' in a few months' time and we'd share the proceeds. Diamond choker: convert. Pearl necklaces: convert. Only I wasn't sure about the pearls. I had a dim memory of Mum giving Fiona and me a list of things and who should have them. It wasn't with her will, it dated further back, around the time she moved out of the Hawkhurst house. I'd searched for it before leaving Sydney, but couldn't find it. I seemed to remember she wanted us to have a pearl necklace each. Fiona said she'd never wear one so I had the 'better' one, with a small diamante clasp.

Mum had so much stuff. Dinner services, a cabinet of crystal glasses of all shapes, vases, coasters, framed antique maps, chairs galore, casseroles ... cupboards stuffed with wrapping paper, notelets, tapestry wool. Much of it Fiona and I did not need, or want. But one thing we'd both thought of when we turned to items we might like were the steam boats. I think my parents must have got them in Hong Kong when we stopped there on the way to Australia. They were brass-coloured, like a small moat suspended over a heating device—a small fuel dish with a flame. Into the 'moat' went stock, and diners took little morsels of fish, vegetables and meat and sat them in the wire baskets in the hot stock until it was cooked. Many a fun meal had been had with them. We looked everywhere for them. The garage—only the car and a wall of firewood; the shed—bins, bits and pieces, nothing 'good'; the cellar—we looked in every cardboard box, every wicker basket, inside my old wardrobe (still with the Chicago Pizza Pie Factory menu Blu-tacked onto one door). Every cupboard in each room. Nowhere. It was particularly odd as Mum hadn't originally taken them from the Hawkhurst house. Then a few months after she moved out she'd sent a mutual friend round for them. Dad knew where they were and had handed them over. We never did find out what she'd done with them.

Once Fiona and I had gone through the main items we wanted, Fiona was keen to get back to Devon and her girls. There was a foul argument with my father. Like the most terrible arguments, it was over something silly. It wasn't really, at the heart of it, even over anything really—just the sort of thing that erupts when there's lots of tension about. Fiona would not stay in the house and said she'd go and sleep at Mum's. Anne was concerned. She didn't like the idea of her alone there. 'What about milk? and something for breakfast?' she asked. I must admit I wasn't keen on sleeping there myself and while I felt perhaps for loyalty's sake I should, I said as much and stayed put at Dad and Anne's. Besides, the quarrel was not mine.

So Fiona slept a night at Mum's and then drove home. It was fine, she said. She'd said before that she didn't feel her presence in the house, that she'd moved elsewhere.

I spent a few days alone in the house—during the day— and her neighbours invited me in for a soup lunch. I took a bottle of wine from Mum's cellar, although we didn't drink it then. They gave me back a history of Europe that Mum had lent them. 'She's still here,' the woman said cheerfully. 'I can still feel her.'

I can't say I 'felt' her, although I liked the little birds tweeting and hopping about on the small trees outside and thought it would be nice if her spirit was still hopping about a bit, enjoying the sunshine and the beauty of the place. But I'm not sure if I'd really have liked to 'feel' her or not—certainly not inside the house, anyway. I did not feel altogether comfortable in her house. As well as gathering in a pile the things I wanted to take back to Australia, I was picking out items for Sheila. I took her a couple of coats, some jumpers, including a pale blue one Mum had been wearing a lot recently and is wearing in one of her last photos, on her sixtieth birthday. Her face is puffy and her skin blotchy. She's smiling broadly but it's slightly forced. She looks tired. The sparkle's still there in her eyes—in some photographs of her in earlier years she has beautiful eyes—but the toughness has gone. I took the oil lamp, which I thought Máire wanted, and a tapestry footstool for Sheila. One with a yellow, patterned background and a grey-and-white cat. It was covered in dust. I also took some wine and champagne to keep at Sheila's for Peter and me to enjoy in years to come. As I loaded all this into the car boot, I felt my heart pounding. I felt furtive and materialistic. I kept having to remind myself that this was what Mum wanted. She was proud of her worldly goods and wanted us to enjoy them after she'd gone. She'd have rather people in the family use them than it all go to charity or auction.

Over the next few days my heart pounded more and more. Even sometimes lying in bed. I realised it was every time I thought of the material side of it all, the 'things'.

But in many other ways it was lovely to be in her house alone. I heard people passing by the kitchen window—voices, skipping feet, the scratchy steps of dogs. What a great place this had been for her. I imagined her here in this house, in the kitchen, cooking lunch, perhaps with the television on. She liked daytime TV, especially cooking shows, so had a TV in the kitchen too. In fact she had four TVs. One in each sitting room, one in the kitchen and a tiny one, not in use, in the bedroom. (Fiona had taken them all to put in her attic and use one by one as they broke down!) I could see why she liked it here.

Village life had suited her. She enjoyed the regular contact with people and had often told me how many people she met when she walked down the high street to the post office.

The rector blew in one morning, looking very dashing in a black cloak. He certainly dressed the part. I thought he might want to console me, perhaps talk of the afterlife. But after I made a cup of tea, noticing that Mum didn't seem to have a teapot anymore, he talked for ages about how hard it was getting in the church, and how the church was selling up property and those in service were having to live in smaller and smaller places.

Hanging in Mum's kitchen window was the crystal bauble I'd given her, purchased one year in the Blue Mountains. Peter had won a door prize of two business-class tickets to Hawaii. It sounded great and I pored through the *Eye Witness Guide to Hawaii* and got quite into the different areas and the day trips you could do. But we couldn't change the tickets to four economy class so in the end Peter went with a friend, who offered to pick up the accommodation costs. I took the boys to the Blue Mountains, to Blackheath. I rented a cabin for a few nights in a holiday park opposite the swimming pool. I took tea and red wine for me, the *Reader's Digest Bumper Book of Games* to keep Harry amused. Felix, then still only one, but walking, was in fine form. We had a couple of bushwalks at Govett's Leap, went on the Gondola across the gully past the Three Sisters and took the Zig Zag Railway. It was a great little holiday.

Maybe it was some time before Christmas. I had been looking for gifts to send to England. We had a crystal hanging in our bathroom and it was magical when the sun came through making tiny rainbows all over the ceiling and walls. The one I chose for Mum was round, with lots of facets, hanging on a chain.

And here it was now. She had hung it in the window facing the high street. It sent rainbows deep into the house, into the large, dark sitting room, onto the ancient bricks of the inglenook fireplace.

When Mum had seen the plans of her cottage, which, way back, had been part of the Swan Inn, it appeared her section had been the kitchen, in which case her enormous fireplace would have been roaring with a pot hanging over it, bubbling away. Mind you, the house and kitchen would have gone through dozens of incarnations since it was built in 1550 or so.

Burwash is full of beautiful old houses. The street had heritage protection, and many houses were listed. Mum's friend Jean had lived in the house opposite, which had a lovely wave to its tiled roof. Another house, Rampyndene, has a mention in Pevsner's *The Buildings of England, Sussex*. (Built in 1699 by a timber merchant. 'The hall has a splendid stucco ceiling with almost detached leaves and flowers,' it notes.)

Mum would have loved to have got inside Rampyndene, with its skewiff but impressive porch, but she never quite managed an invitation. It was the lady at Rampyndene, though, who'd noticed that Mum's bedroom curtains hadn't been drawn that Wednesday morning. During the days I was alone at Burwash, I went to see her. To say hello? To thank her for her assistance that morning? To return something ... She told me that she'd noticed the curtains weren't pulled back, which was unusual for Mum. Then at 1 pm she'd noticed Jackie arrive but appear to have difficulty getting in. Jackie would normally go in the back door, which Mum would have opened, but I guess when she found it closed, she tried knocking at the front, on the high street. The lady from Rampyndene had gone over, I think, and suggested Jackie call the doctors' from their house. The doctor had said 'call an ambulance' and soon afterwards Mum was found, curled up, seemingly asleep, peaceful, I imagine, in her bed. The ambulance officers had to break in through a tiny bathroom window at the back. I suppose they lifted her onto a stretcher, covered her body and carried her out to the ambulance. 'I thought your mum was much older than sixty,' the lady said to me. 'Many people would like to go the way she did—in her sleep,' she added kindly.

I invited Jackie round for a cup of tea. I warned her that Fiona and I had started to dismantle the house, taking pictures off the walls and things out of cupboards and off shelves. I guessed it would be a shock to see the house in disarray. It was always so neat when Mum lived there. Jackie came to Mum's house twice a week over several years and would have heard all about her trials, tribulations and plans ... I asked her if when she took on the job as home help, they'd said anything about her drinking. Jackie nodded. 'They did mention she'd had a problem with it ... but she was very discreet, wasn't she?' Well, yes, she was hardly throwing wild parties, or staggering about in public. She kept her habit pretty private.

Jackie repeated how she'd come to the house around 1

pm and couldn't get in. After the ambulance was called, she'd gone home. 'Then I heard the ambulance siren coming up the high street.' I hadn't thought of that before—the standard emergency, not knowing what they'd find, the reaction of the infrastructure to a death at home alone. All that noise and adrenalin for someone who'd already died, in their sleep, some time before.

I showed her some pictures of Mum when she was younger. There was one of her around my age, very slim and tanned, wearing one of the print dresses that was folded in her cupboard. Straps over the shoulder, black with small curling flowers in orange and red. She was holding a glass and talking to someone at a party in Egypt. 'She was very elegant,' Jackie commented.

I checked that Jackie had been paid up to date. 'Oh yes, she was always very good about that.'

I asked Jackie if she'd like one of Mum's tapestries. 'Oh yes, that would be lovely.' Did she have a favourite? Was there one she particularly liked? She didn't want to choose, so I gave her a recent one that Mum had done, in a sampler style, a large one. I knew neither Fiona nor I wanted it, and it was a special one. Jackie deserved that. She was thrilled with it. We hugged briefly on saying goodbye. 'She was a lovely lady,' Jackie said to me. 'A lovely lady ... '

�֍

Mum was difficult to buy gifts for. Yet, especially once she lived alone, they assumed a greater importance. You wouldn't want to miss a birthday or Christmas when the people in her comfort zone had dwindled so much. In part I found her difficult because I couldn't help thinking that she would buy herself anything she really coveted—which didn't leave us much room for manoeuvre in the gift department. In a way we all labelled her as materialistic— and didn't the fact that she had a house crammed with goods, but was alone, while Dad had been left with almost bare walls, but had a companion, prove it? But she lived on a modest income those last years. She was a careful and accurate budgeter. She wasn't really extravagant. What did she buy? Books ... expensive fish cuts occasionally, wine, no doubt, clothes—often from mail order. But she lived well within her new means and left her financial and legal affairs in impeccable order.

She was often critical of gifts she didn't like but felt compelled to display them.

She appreciated an extravagant gesture, however. For her birthday following the one she'd spent in hospital, when I sent her that copy of Stephanie Alexander's *A Cook's Companion,* with the orange cloth spine almost three inches wide, Mum had shown off the postage label as much as the book itself.

Fiona and I had an unspoken agreement that if we'd given Mum something ourselves, we had first choice over it. I took back a red beaded and embroidered bag; a bone-handled miniature pewter ladle; a small, long Indian box with an antiqued bird. I also claimed a beautifully smooth, carved bird with a long tail that I knew Dad had given her one recent birthday, and which I knew meant a lot to her. She was chuffed that he remembered, even though they had no other contact.

Mum was a mail-order queen. Her pine chest in the little sitting room (where you'd often hear birds chirping at the top of the chimney) always had a new catalogue on it. She liked to choose gifts for the family from them as well as items for herself. I'd often receive little clippings of a bath toy with water wheel, or other toy telling me in advance what she'd ordered for the boys' gifts.

'I've got yours, Fiona, the boys' presents for next year and the year after,' she told me once with pride. She undoubtedly was well ahead of me; I tend to get anxious a couple of weeks before Christmas Day itself. She appeared to have done much of her Christmas shopping already the week she died. But that year the present-hoarding had stopped. Fiona and I went through every shelf and drawer but while there were some items which looked like presents tucked away for the future, there weren't that many. She had told me, towards the end of the year we'd had in England, that she didn't think she had much time left, 'A year, maybe ... ' she'd said. 'Not much longer.' Well, she turned out to be spot-on. Had she stopped buying ahead too?

While I was over for Mum's funeral, Dad's horse was lame and it was hunting season. Or was he still recovering from a broken rib? One way or another, he was not riding but was going to follow the hunt. I came too. The day promised lots of walking across fields, a bit of adventure and gallons of fresh air and English countryside. I've been to lots of meets—the gathering of the riders that will follow the hounds and their leaders, the hunt officials, some of whom wear red woollen jackets known as hunting pink. The dogs sniff around, tails in the air, with an optimistic, 'life is simple' look about them. The horsy folk come in several varieties: ones with well-off accents and the latest in boots/ horse rugs/hats; the ones that scrape together all they can to keep a horse; the asset-rich, cash-poor semi-aristocrats with threadbare gear but glowing confidence. There's chat, exchange of horsy gossip, 'Gosh, I haven't seen you for ages ... ', talk of so-and-so's lame horse, someone else's fall, what regulations have to be surmounted for the up-and-coming cross-country day.

Eventually it's time to set off. The hunt is organised and the pinks together. The bugle is sounded and away they go. Dogs eager. Riders enthusiastic. Usually a slow pace to begin with. And lots of waiting around for dogs to do their business. Early on, the riders had to stand in a field while the huntsmen and dogs went sniffing around on the hedged marshes. Dad and I, being on foot, could go nearer the action. We were standing in a car-wide track, a flat field on one side, a tall tangled hedge on the other. The hunt and their dogs were in a far corner, 50 metres or so away. Suddenly a reddish blond streak of a creature came hurtling towards us, eyes keen, legs like the wind. It dived into the hedge and out the other side into another small field. A huntsman came galloping up behind, calling the dogs. They came bumbling along noses down, smelling every blade of grass but they seemed fairly hopeless. The fox had gone into a tiny patch of woodland between a couple of fields, behind a wooden fence. The dogs were called over there and ran under the fence, between the trees, over and around a little earthy mound. 'He's gone to ground,' the huntsmen said after a while. Dad and I stood near the fence. I'd never been this close to a fox while hunting. I'd hunted a couple of times but my only experience was riding into the unknown—where we were going, would there be jumps, gallops?—and some jumping, occasionally a fall. It was an exciting day's riding, more often than not without a kill. And even if there was, you didn't see anything, it all happened some distance off.

This fox had found a hole, squeezed into it and the dogs were too big to follow. They were called off and the riders went elsewhere, while guys on foot took over. Wearing tweedy jackets, caps or oilskins, they climbed over the fence. One or two were carrying spades, another had a pistol.

I suddenly felt disgusted and if I didn't move away from the scene, that I might burst into tears. Seeing the spades, the earth, thinking of the persecuted creature about to be hauled from its hiding place was all too much. Especially just a day or so after seeing my mother's grave dug in the earth. The ultimate hounding, it seemed, was without a hound in sight. From the point of view of the activity, it seemed one thing to do it 'by the rules', with dogs and speed and trails of scent, but quite another with human cunning, man-made shovels and guns.

'I don't think I can watch this,' I said to Dad. We moved off.

'Controlled aggression' is how I saw the hunt that day. There were three guys following the hunt in an official capacity, on a quad bike. They were in it for the kills and carried the corpses in a bag at the front. One, Dad said, had an evil reputation and a violent streak. Maybe it was just as well they did a bit of this rather than fighting at the pub?

Mum took a distant interest in hunting. Dad's setting off to the meets had been part of her life for years. She'd sometimes helped him load a stubborn horse and once or twice driven with the trailer. One of the cuttings she'd been about to send me was about the protests in London over the banning of hunting.

Once I'd picked out the things I would ship back to Australia, I thought of what I could usefully do in the house that would be one less job for Fiona. I took a black garbage bag and emptied into it underwear, tights, nighties from drawers and shelves in Mum's bedroom. Things neither Fiona nor I wanted, yet seemed too personal for the charity shop or for house clearers to handle. Mum would like the extra touch of dignity, I thought. Ditto the bathroom and wicker baskets of creams and make-up.

Despite the fact she wasn't always the greatest eater, Mum's cupboards were full of food. It seemed such a waste, but I didn't know where to start with local organisations that might want tins and unopened packets. Mum's neighbour Nicky said she'd find a home for it all if I would gather it all together. 'I don't want to go through your mum's cupboards,' she explained.

There were mail orders that arrived after Mum died.

Some may have been destined for Christmas presents, but we didn't like to presume. So we had to return them. Mostly we had to include copies of the death certificate.

Nicky was great. She came into the house for weeks, opening and closing curtains, filling the bird feeder for quite a while too. I had planned to remove the flowers covering Mum's grave on my last day there. I wasn't looking forward to the task but preferred that over a neglected mass of flowers slowly rotting. But Nicky said she'd do it and it turned out the flowers looked good for another three weeks.

I paid a visit to Clare, the elderly lady Mum had befriended, for whom she'd done lots of little favours, whether looking after her dog, picking up prescriptions or taking to casualty. Mum had been looking after, too, a small bundle of Clare's silverware that Fiona had had to hunt down and return before it got muddled up in the disposal of Mum's possessions. Clare invited me into her cottage and I sat for a short while talking. My mother had been very tired in the last few months, she said. Perhaps she hinted at being tired of it all. Clare seemed to say Mum was due a checkup but didn't want to go through with it. She seemed to suggest that although happy in many ways, she'd also quite simply had enough. It made sense. Her heart condition really put the brakes on and made the simplest of things a big task. She'd had to pace herself and force herself to do things that seemed like nothing to the rest of us. She'd done far more than anyone imagined she could after her diagnosis. But she couldn't go on forever.

I paid a last visit to Mum's grave. The stone would not be in place for several months yet but a small black marker held her name and dates. I walked around the churchyard. There was a commemorative chair for a young girl, Jean Maude Roxby's elegant stone (Mum's friend who had lived opposite Cygnet Cottage), ancient tombs dating back hundreds of years, their names worn with the centuries.

Mum carried many secrets to her grave. The steam boats among them! Who knows what else. The rest of us had our secrets too. Fiona's concerned Daisy. She was a cocker spaniel, black and white. A bundle of energy and affection. She'd gone with Mum to Burwash and at first Mum had taken her for walks through the churchyard and into the fields. Then some time when Mum became ill, I guess before her crisis, it had become too much. Fiona said she'd find a home for Daisy and the story went she'd found a family nearby to take her. She might even have had her at home herself for a little while. But in fact, it was Pat and Owen who took the dog, and were really happy to have her. Mum had cut Pat and Owen off—they were possibly her oldest friends. They'd taken their babies to the clinic together, swapped babysitting, I'd gone to Pat's nursery school, she and Pat had been in the poetry group together. She cut them off like she cut off nearly everyone from her 'old' life. I think when she and Dad split up she wanted a fresh start for one. Owen had taken her out to lunch once and phoned Dad afterwards to say how worried he was about Eleanor. It had got back to her and that was that. She had great pride and found it difficult to navigate relationships that crossed boundaries.

A major secret that we all kept was the fact that Mum's sisters kept in contact with Dad. When Mum turned sixty, she'd arranged for the gang—Sheila, Máire and John, Fiona, Hope and Harriet—to go out for lunch. They usually split the bill, but this time Máire had insisted she pay. Mum had been quite surprised and had written telling me. Máire's secret, that she could tell us but Mum was not to know, was that Dad had given her money to pay for the lunch.

While I was over for the year, during a visit or maybe in those first few months when we were in Kent, I was in the passenger seat of Dad's car, driving down the high street in Burwash. I remember seeing Mum. In my mind's eye she is almost striding. She was wearing a white jumper with a navy V-neck and jeans. She saw us and flashed a big smile towards the car. 'She doesn't look as bad as I thought,' said

Dad, who'd not seen her since she had become so ill, and had only heard stories of her predicament. I later said to her what a lovely smile she'd given us. 'The smile was for you,' she said.

In my last morning with Dad the breakfast table was set as usual. Dad got out a shoebox of photos. There were pictures going back over the decades during various life stages: 'before she got ill', 'when her drinking started to get bad'. In a couple of pictures of them in Egypt she looked so pretty and full of life, shoulder-length hair, she was talking to someone and laughing. I hadn't really cried with Dad around—Dad had done his weeping before I arrived and we took the 'let's button up' option once I was there. But I'd done enough holding in. As we looked at photo after photo and the odd little detail came out about his family, about Mum, what it was like, I couldn't stop the tears anymore. They just rolled down my face, one after another, silently. Dad didn't say anything either and we continued to go through the box of photos.

Dad was to drive me up to Sheila's a day or so before my flight back to Australia. I wanted to spend a bit of time with her and take her out to dinner. I needed to return Mum's car to her garage. Fiona would pick it up later with a friend. So I took the car back and parked it in the garage, then had a final walk around Mum's house. I hated the feeling that it was the last time. We'd already started dismantling it, but it was still her home. Most objects had been put in their place years ago and stood there still. There were objects from all the different eras of her life. A set of brass mugs from Egypt. Attractive enough. What would become of them? Paintings of ships that had been on the walls of our family home. The sitting room where she'd sew, listen to sad music, fill the bird feeder. As I came down the stairs I noticed a tiny stoneware bird. It was a style I'd seen many times. Had it been mine? Had Dad given it to her? I picked it up, put it in my coat pocket and left.

Sheila showed me photographs she had of Mum. On a tricycle as a child; a black-and-white studio portrait when she was fourteen, wearing knobbly beads I remember being in our dress-up box by the time we were toddlers; aunts in nuns' habits crossing a river, their dresses pulled up to their knees! It was lovely to talk about her. I took Sheila out to dinner. We walked along the towpath by the Thames, past the houseboats, the ducks and geese, the river dark and swirling.

For some reason, I found it hard to take everything that I wanted from Mum's house. There was a flowered breakfast set that Auntie Isabel had given her as a wedding present. I thought I'd give it to Sheila, then asked her to keep it for me until my next visit.

Sheila asked, 'Do you think families are reunited in heaven? I'm wondering if Eleanor will be with Mummy and Daddy now.' I looked at her, barely concealing a laugh. 'I don't know,' I replied, thinking what a nightmare it could be if you hadn't got on with someone in life, only to find yourself forced together again for eternity.

The time came for me to leave. My shipment had gone. I'd seen Mum one more time, the funeral had gone well, Fiona and I had chosen the stone for her tombstone. Dad had made a beautiful job of wrapping the painting. I was missing my own boys like mad. 'I even feel like being pestered and irritated!' I joked to a friend. Peter warned me that the house looked like 'God has vomited on it.' It didn't matter. Wasn't important. It was time to go home.

Heading back, my suitcase was fuller than on the way over and I had the painting of the boys at the beach to carry as hand luggage. I fronted up at the airline check-in desk to a beautifully groomed, slim and attractive black lady with short hair. 'Madam, you have an allowance of twenty kilograms and you have thirty-six,' she told me, expressionless.

'I'm sorry,' I said matter-of-factly, 'I've been over for my mother's funeral and have taken a few things back from her house.' She didn't flinch, but checked the bags through without a further word. No one batted an eyelid at the excellently wrapped painting and it fitted in the overhead locker without a problem. I was on my way home.

FOUR

THE EXPAT LIFE

Cairo was dirty, chaotic and exotic. Frogs croaked from drains at night and calls to prayer caterwauled from the minarets. Near the airport, there were people living in dumps, picking through the rubbish for something to sell. The streets were crammed with honking cars, plodding donkeys, bicycles, buses and motorbikes. Crossing the road was an art.

Mum and Dad decided to live in Maadi, an expatriate suburb of Cairo that must once have been glorious. It still had some beautiful buildings and tree-lined streets, but there were broken pavements and holes in the dusty road.

They rented a spacious but quite modest apartment with big arched windows, tiled floors and noisy air conditioning units in the bedrooms. From the windows you could watch the sun set over Maadi's palm trees.

I remember the first time I visited. This was the early eighties. I stepped out of the plane onto the flight of steps they used then. I felt a blast of hot air and looked out into the Egyptian night, the twinkling lights of a distant city, wondering what the darkness held.

Later, half asleep in bed, I heard frogs croaking through the night and dreamt of camels walking through the streets.

In Cairo, everywhere you looked there was something going on: talking, haggling, begging. People's emotions seemed to run at a higher level. When they tried to cross the teeming streets in the middle of the city, they adopted a pleading gesture with their hands, as if holding something small between all their fingertips, and moving it back and forwards for all to see.

On the outskirts of the city, my parents pointed out blocks of flats that had additional floors put on top, so landlords could extract more money. These additions would come without additional foundations, and terrible accidents, when they tumbled down, were not uncommon.

Maadi was an oasis of calm compared to the hubbub of the city centre. At my parents' block of flats was a caretaker, Said, who when on duty slept in a room hardly any bigger than a cupboard. He was very dark and seemed old, with deep crow's-feet wrinkles around his eyes, but he was strong. He carried our mahogany dining table up four flights of stairs on his head. He asked Dad if he could have the packing boxes from the shipment. Mum and Dad said he was taking them for bedding. Said wore a dark buttoned shirt and trousers often rolled halfway up his stocky calves. He had little, if any, English, but a ready, white smile that flashed with a few gaps.

Mum and Dad plunged enthusiastically into the expat life. They joined the local club—where you could have a drink (but seeing trolleys laden with large blocks of ice, barely covered with a piece of cotton, you might choose to avoid ice), play squash and swim. It was on a large block of land in Maadi with enough space for people to ride horses and to put on an annual showjumping competition.

As was the done thing among their contemporaries, they hired a maid, Suhair. She was a fleshy, smiling lady in traditional attire. She'd mop the cool tiles in her bare feet, revealing a spare little toe. She was Coptic, which meant time off in January for the Coptic Christmas.

They also hired a cook, but she didn't last long as the food she made was unpalatable. Rock-hard cakes, tough meat ...

Mum was a good cook but it took a little while for her to learn to deal with local ingredients as well as local shopping. The meat market was indoors, with blood-dripping carcasses hanging on all sides in a moist and darkened atmosphere. I went there once with her. It was no place for the squeamish. The meat wasn't hung to season it like in England, jane l so tended to be tougher. After a while Mum learnt that if you froze the meat for six months, it became tender. She soaked vegetables in chlorinated water before putting them in the fridge and boiled the drinking water—all in an effort to reduce the chance of getting any of the many bugs that laid foreigners down low. It was best to avoid lettuce, people told her, because of the large surface area of the leaves and the difficulty of really cleaning it.

You could buy fruit and vegetables on 'Road 9', Maadi's dusty shopping street. Tomatoes bigger than tennis balls and bulging cucumbers. You could also get groceries there, like cereals and milk, and, if you needed it, there were shops crammed with rolls of fabric lining the walls behind a large counter. Then there was the 'Step-down-store' where you could have clothes copied. (This quickly became quite a preoccupying pastime for my mother.) Expats also had perks like a monthly allowance at the duty-free shop on alcohol, cigarettes for friends (neither of my parents smoked) and imported clothes.

Once out of your cool apartment, everything was different. Well, of course, it was you who was different. You had paler skin and were wealthier. Eyes would follow you down the street. Swarms of children would emerge from nowhere with constant demands for baksheesh (money). Even at the museum, police in uniform would whisper, 'Psst ... you want change money?' One of the skills you learnt there was the ability to keep walking, say no, and look straight ahead.

Although winter days could be surprisingly cool, it was the heat you really noticed compared to England. It could get hot—over 100 degrees—but usually it was dry, so it was quite bearable. But in letters home to me, there was always something to say about the weather: 'It's been really strange this last week,' Mum wrote one week. 'Very humid. The hygrometer was reading 85% humidity—which for here is really high. Suhair was really hot and the little tailor said it was very dangerous weather!'

Then there was the Khamsin, the oppressive hot and dusty wind that came in from the south. One night the landlord's daughter came to ask them to close their shutters as the ones on the third floor had blown off. They shut them, but not before thick grey dust had come into every room of the house.

Being dropped into an expatriate corporate community, there was a ready-made circle of friends. Sudden new acquaintances to share the experience of strangeness and privilege: families of people working for the same company as Dad, as well as contractors. Americans, English, Canadians, Germans. A big-boned German lady called Renate who was allergic to the combination of proteins found in ice cream and mangoes. Nellwyn, with immaculate clothes, a tall and slim Texan with the drawl to go with it; Helga, a petite pretty German; a homely American couple, Hazel and Harold. A few young couples with babies, many semi-empty-nesters like my parents who had children at boarding school or university visiting in the holidays.

There was a constant flow of new people. Newcomers' coffee mornings, farewell dinners, invitations to write and arrangements to make. There were dinner parties, drinks parties, invitations to restaurants.

> … last night we went to Joe and Salwa's. They had what they liked to call an 'international set'—there was an Egyptian actress and producer (very famous apparently), an Egyptian ambassador, a gay Englishman who's with the New York Herald Tribune, plus a couple of Embassy people and a few company ones. The gay chap admired my coral twisted with my pearls and thought they were awfully nice and very clever!

Then there were the sorties in the night to tents with belly dancers.

We had a really late night on Thursday—3.30 am! When we were at the Salters the other week Dad was going on about belly dancers to Mr Z, an Egyptian, so much so that Mr Z arranged a night out at an Egyptian nightclub. I wasn't exactly pleased, especially when we arranged to meet at 11.30!! Dino and Françoise were invited as well, which helped. We met D and F at Swiss Air (upstairs) at 8.30 for dinner and then went on to El Lil (the nightclub) at 11.30. Of course they had food there and we had to eat again! Mr Z kept giving Dad lamb chops and he had six!

There were wives' luncheons to go to and new bosses to show around. Once, they went to a cocktail party given by a drilling company. The drilling 'set' was quite different, Mum told me. 'These drillers and their wives are really "loud and brassy". Horrible really!'

The Cairo Players put on *A Man for All Seasons*, and, in a private garden, a production of Monty Python's *Life of Brian*, in semi-secret because it might have upset the strong Christian element in the expats. The British Embassy hosted *The Malesh Revue* with drinks, supper and sketches. The Petroleum Wives put on a fashion show at the Hilton ('most of the clothes were awful and the models were a bit "stiff" ').

I was in London at this time and Fiona at boarding school in Kent, so our lives became more independent of each other. But we all wrote often, Mum and Dad usually writing on a Sunday (in a letter usually started by one and finished by the other), putting a letter in the company mail pouch. The letters are full of the details that made up their lives then. They are full, too, of the concerns of a family split up geographically. Tell us when your exams are, did you get your bike brakes fixed? What are you going to do for the long weekend? If you go down to Hawkhurst, can you give the car a spin, but don't forget to disconnect the battery again when you leave, otherwise it will run down.

When I think back on my mother during the years in Egypt, I think of a busy person, enjoying the challenges of setting up in a new city. She no doubt liked the status of the 'frills' that came with being an executive expat's wife: having a maid, hiring waiters for drinks parties, going to expensive restaurants. In our letters we shared lots of facts, but perhaps not so much feeling. My university days were not entirely happy ones, but I'm not sure how much of that I shared with either of my parents at the time.

Every now and then they'd make a phone call from the company office by satellite. It was quite a performance, you may even have had to book to use the phone. When Granny Mac became sick, Mum called Máire once a week to find out how she was, and when she succumbed to breast cancer and died, Mum went back to London for the funeral.

There was a toing and froing of requests: to check a dentist's appointment; Mum wanted some pop socks; music tapes, what she called, 'the usual stuff; Fleetwood Mac, Simon & Garfunkel etc. Got The Beatles.' Visiting dates were a major issue. 'Don't forget to let us know your dates and arrival times' was a frequent ending to the weekly letters. 'Don't forget a piece of holly for the pudding.'

There were comings and goings, especially in school holidays. Relatives and friends taking advantage of somewhere to stay and visit. Airport arrivals were often met with a company car and a meeter and greeter to help visitors through the airport queues. (A regular one had shocking teeth. He told us how much he liked sugar, even with chicken.) There were often delays, planes two hours late arriving, delayed departures too. Thin cats wandered round the airport. The drive to Maadi could be rough: there were major potholes which would either be swerved round or bumped over, sending our heads up to the car roof.

There was lots to show visitors. The Son et Lumière at the pyramids was so good Mum and Dad saw it three times. Visitors liked the shopping too. The Khan el-Khalili was a favourite place for us all. A seething, winding mass of lanes with tiny stalls and shops, just a few people wide, where you'd practise your bargaining. When it came to bartering, we'd often try the walk-away technique. It usually brought prices crashing—whether for checked cotton Arabian scarves or silver jewellery.

Buying perfume was a special performance. And quite a treat. First tea was ordered. Strong black peppermint tea, brought with lots of sugar already in it. Served in thick glasses on a brass tray. The shop would be small with tall cabinets along the walls, filled with bottles. The proprietor might wear a long tunic called a galabeyah or a loose shirt over trousers. He'd smear little drops of attar of roses, or essence of jasmine on your wrist, your lower arm, and you'd come away with little bottles of sweet-smelling, thick, oily perfume.

Mum took Sheila to the Khan el-Khalili and wrote later:

> We went to the perfume shop and had some tea
> while we tried the various perfumes. He's my friend,
> the owner! He's also about 80! He kissed my hand
> and asked us if we'd like tea and sent out for it. He
> then put essence of mint in it and the smell was
> fantastic—it cleared one's head just like smelling

salts ... We felt obliged to buy some perfume, it's only a few pounds, so it's not much. He posed for a photo for Sheila.

There was lots to explore. After a visit to the museum with its Tutankhamen treasures, people would exchange horror stories of seeing a drip of water in a cabinet containing a millennia-old chair or statue that to our Western minds should have been climate controlled for preservation. The mummies were still on display there; soon afterwards they were removed from view.

And of course, the pyramids at Giza. Sometimes people were surprised, and perhaps disappointed that they were so near the city. They are right, bang, at its edge, the sprawling city having gradually crept closer and closer, no doubt. But I loved seeing them. At dawn, on the way to the riding school a kilometre or so from the pyramids, at sunset after a day's sightseeing, in the distance from a taxi, up close when you were visiting them.

We climbed to the top one morning. A friend of Dad's had organised it. You needed a guide, as it could be treacherous. Several people had died from falls off the pyramids. So a guide would show the best, safest route up and down. And you had to give bribe money to the right people in the police, too. Mum did not come with us (perhaps, neither did other mothers). It was mainly for the young people, in our teens and twenties.

I seem to remember about twenty of us gathering in the pre-dawn dark. As you were not officially allowed to climb the pyramids, climbs were arranged well before the tourists arrived each day. It was cool and misty. After last-minute 'discussions' with various Egyptians in shabby uniforms, we were allowed to go.

A yellow-grey sun rose in the dusty sky as we climbed the Great Pyramid, which we called Cheops. Once, it had a smooth facing all over, like the top of the next pyramid, Kephren, but that has worn off, so instead, its surface is of huge, 1.5-ton stone blocks. We scrambled up each one, taking about half an hour to reach the top. From the ground, the top looks pointy, but in fact, there's the floor space of a large room up there   I'm tempted to say 'like a small ballroom' because I feel like we were not unsimilar to the aristocratic tourists who travelled in the nineteenth and early twentieth century. It was crammed with engraved initials and dates.

You could look out into the desert, or back towards the city of Cairo. The mist and dust had not cleared, so you could not see very far, but the pyramid complex itself was clear, including an amazing view of Kephren, looking so solid from this angle.

Mum didn't climb it, but she read up on all the history and we all learnt the names: Cheops, Kephren and Mycerinos.

We would ride around the pyramids and the Sphinx sometimes, on beautiful Arab horses from the stables. I remember once a small yellow plane zipping in and around, buzzing in the air.

One of the best riding experiences was to the step pyramid at Saqqara. You'd leave at 4 am in a party of half a dozen or even a dozen and start in the dark. We'd ride through the desert, past unnamed graveyards and falling-down, smaller pyramids. They'd loom up in the distance, then suddenly you'd be on them and passing right by. On shorter rides, we'd have a gallop over the undulating sand, but on these ones, you'd save your horse's energy. Our guides would be wearing galabeyahs and headgear like Lawrence of Arabia, chatting to us, asking us about London, or university, practising their English or French. For some of the time we'd ride by small villages with single-storey buildings, many made of mud. The ride would take several hours and at the destination Mum and other non-riders would meet us with a breakfast of watermelon, thin slices of cheese, bread rolls and coffee.

There was a fairly ready-made circle of friends for my sister and me. Sons and daughters of Mum's and Dad's friends, often coming and going just like us. There were day trips to the Club Med, parties, outings to discos in the large hotels. The city was considered safe, so we'd travel by taxi, often in groups. There was quite an art to taking taxis. It was not a question of simply hailing one. Locals went by the meter and shared. Foreigners did not expect to share, but in return were expected to pay more. The usual practice was to barter for your fare before you got in. So you had to make yourself understood. One, where you were going and two, how much you were prepared to pay. Sometimes, your handful of Arabic words was not enough and they couldn't work out where you wanted to go.

Some of Mum's friends and acquaintances had drivers, which was always an easy option to getting around. You could risk the train but the buses were a definite no-no. They were filled to the gunnels and you'd sometimes see people climbing in back windows. If they crashed, the loss of life would be high, simply because they were so full.

We all enjoyed new eating experiences in Egypt. Hotels were air-conditioned havens from the dust and chaos of the streets. There you'd find a clean toilet, a soft seat for coffee or a piled-high buffet for lunch and dinner. Local restaurants had more colour, more interesting menus and more ambience, but also more chance of food poisoning.

Food poisoning stories were high up on topics of conversation whenever a group of foreigners gathered. We all watched a waiter in horror once at club called The Good Shot, on a lovely spot by the Nile where white-sailed feluccas glided by. We had been enjoying a cool drink and a few plates of thinly spread houmous and bread. There was the waiter, in his cotton jacket and trouser uniform, taking used glasses off the table, wiping them with a tea towel, and placing them with no further ado, back on the 'clean' glasses section of the serving table.

You had to laugh at it, but you didn't laugh when you were up in the middle of the night.

Mum enjoyed eating in restaurants, the more expensive the better as far as she was concerned. Usually these occasions were invitations from work people '... we were taken out to dinner in the evening. We went to the Palme d'Or restaurant at the Meridien which is expensive and not bad. But not as good as Swiss Air. Tonight we're off to the Corporals' Club ... It's the British Community Club where you can get egg and chips or something and watch a film.'

Sometimes a few families might take a felucca ride at sunset. It felt glamorous and exotic, sitting in the slim elegant boats with their beautiful, simple white sails. But you'd be hoping you didn't fall in as the Nile was infested with snails that could give you a dreadful disease called bilharzia.

There were barbecue parties in the desert, near magnificent gorges with wind-sculpted sandstone cliffs. There'd be explorations of the rock formations then music and dancing.

Further afield was Ismailia, on the Suez Canal. We'd stop to buy tangerines from the roadside stalls on the way. Once there, if you lay back in the water, you could hear the engines of passing ships rumbling through the depths.

Sometimes Mum joined short trips with other ladies, sometimes at the invitation of contractors associated with Dad's work. Like the trip to Port Said where she boarded a 'millionaire type' yacht to travel through the Suez Canal, arriving a few days later in Ein Sukhna. They decided to stay on the boat to Hurghada, further south, and were supposed to fly back. But because it was an ocean-going vessel, they got caught up in immigration procedures on going ashore and missed the plane. There wasn't a flight the next day. Dad wrote, 'It's almost as if they've been kidnapped. She's been gone one week.'

Mum was obviously very chuffed at the trip and sent me a postcard on her return:

Thought you'd like to see the super yacht I've just left! Got back about 2 o'clock today. Had the most fantastic trip. Beautiful boat, owned by an American millionaire. It's left in Antibes, S France, but the owner is going to do some diving at Hurghada. We joined it at Port Said last Sunday. He arrives in the next few days. From Suez onwards there were just 3 of us and a crew of 8! We had 2 stewards looking after us and were really living in luxury. The boat is worth about $7 million!! It's really beautiful and we all had private bathrooms etc. The weather was very windy and rough until last night and when we left this morning the sea was like a millpond, we were anchored in 12 ft of water and we could see the bottom and all the coral and little fish. We didn't want to leave!

Longer breaks for the two of them could mean a few days in Upper Egypt, confusingly southern Egypt geographically. There was Aswan, Luxor and Abu Simbel. There was the oasis at El Fayoum and the National Arabian Stud where the five top stallions were paraded.

Day-to-day life was harder than in England. There were power cuts and sometimes the water would be off for a couple of hours. It was hard to find places. Mum and Dad had ordered a sculpted head from a man called Hasan

Hashmat (the head, in his realist style in a black stone, reminded them of the caretaker, Said) whose studio was behind Ein Sham station. When due to pick it up, they gave up after three hours of looking. It took two hours to find the butcher that someone had recommended in Old Maadi.

In one letter back to England, Mum told me:

I had to have a major sort out of food this week as we had 'sousse' (in Arabic) in the larder. That's what Suhair said they were and we don't know what they are in English. They are a little tiny insect that were in the lasagne, spaghetti, soup packets etc. Anything in a packet, even foil ones. So I had to throw a lot of stuff away as there were grubs in them! It was horrible. All the rice that I had on the food order has had to go in the freezer and tea bags and nuts. The freezer is bulging at the sides practically now that the meat is added.

Dad found he could ride at the club in Maadi and he went almost every day, taking his own bridle and saddle. Mum took swimming lessons from Ibrahim, who after ninety-two years in the sun, had tanned skin like a lizard. She was forty by then but had never learnt to swim. It wasn't long before he told her that there was not much more he could do for her, it was now up to her. 'I go about 8 strokes from the steps and do my crawl to the steps. I suppose it's a question of building up my confidence and going farther each time.'

We all liked a tan—and it was just before people became more aware about the dangers of the sun—so working on your tan at the club was a major pastime. It was there that Mum made an Egyptian friend called Nadia. Mum was flabbergasted one day when she'd invited Nadia for lunch at about 12. By 1 pm, she'd given up on her, and was fairly stunned when Nadia arrived at 1.30 with the statement, 'You said come about twelve, so I thought I'd come now.' It was her introduction to Egyptian time.

One of the pastimes was having clothes made. It was very cheap, and—with all the choosing of styles and rolls of fabric—it was also entertaining. There was Isis in Old Maadi who made Arabian waistcoats in shiny stripy material for the front and with a thick cotton back, with dozens of tiny knotted buttons down the front. There was the place in the Khan el-Khalili which made galabeyahs, that Nellwyn the Texan introduced Mum to. Mum had a heavy silk one made in case she had to go to a dance, since she hadn't brought any long dresses with her. It was a rich blue with a white trim.

We had very little contact with Egyptians really, apart from perfunctory exchanges with shopkeepers or taxi drivers. Our cultural differences were apparent in all sorts of ways. The painters painted right over the kitchen cupboards so you couldn't open them; Dad gained a reputation for shouting at work; we heard about a man who met an Egyptian lady on a plane and invited her out to dinner. When he asked a second time, her father called to ask his intentions. Did he intend to marry her? (He had to think quick, and decided—yes—he did!) We also heard about a Western woman being courted and charmed by an Egyptian man, but when they married, the tables turned and she was expected to be a traditional Egyptian housewife with little outside life.

The landlord would present a plate of delicious crescent-shaped shortbreads at various feast times. We were invited to the his daughter's wedding. There was music from two bands, a colourful tent, sword dancers, skirt twirlers, limbo dancers, and lots of food. And the shrieking, wailing noise the bride's women attendants made.

Once, when I was visiting, we all visited the Old City, an area with lots of family tombs where sometimes people—having nowhere else—made homes. It smelt of warm, rotting rubbish; that sweet, sickly smell you came across a lot in Cairo. And look! There was an ice cream factory amongst all the grime. It was a brand we often bought; they had a way of making the ice cream very white. Pure. Not like where it was made. There were rivulets of water leaking around it, the building was filthy. I'm not sure we bought the ice cream again.

Some of the lanes were only just wide enough to push a hand cart down. There were markets. Feathery chickens squawking in a wire cage. A freshly killed chicken on the ground, its blood spilling into the grey dirt.

Then a terrible wailing noise. We pushed to the side of the thoroughfare. A man was being carried by a group of men, screaming and writhing in grief, behind him a funeral procession.

Poverty was highly visible, especially in those drives to and from the airport. Maadi was relatively free of beggars, but in other crowded areas, there were cripples and beggars of all ages.

As expats you almost existed in a kind of bubble. So much was self-contained: the friends, some of the shops even, hotels. Other people came into the bubble, and sometimes you made contact or had an experience outside of it, but you were hardly an integrated member of local society. The head of the riding school asked Dad to bring a saddle back from England once. Suhair brought her daughter to visit Mum once. Small, human exchanges, but rare ones.

Mum liked doing tapestries. I think it was in Egypt that she completed one of my favourites, a naive picture of a girl holding a toy, with a black cat in a background like a jungle. I have it in my sitting room now. But at one time she decided that rather than start another tapestry, she'd do something more useful, so knitted baby clothes for the Giza baby clinic. 'I've done four booties and one and a half bonnets this week. I've now run out of wool and will have to get some more tomorrow. I had the wool given to me for the knitting and it's emerald green! The choice was orange, red, brilliant yellow or the green. I thought the green was the best of the bunch. They like bright colours here.'

Mum took Arabic classes at the American University in Cairo (AUC): 'the hardest but the best.' Classes were at the Maadi Yacht Club on the Corniche, the main road leading into central Cairo. Some of the language filtered through without the lessons: *malesh* (never mind), *inshallah* (if God wills it), *baksheesh* (tip money), the numbers (*wahad, etnayn* ...).

She also took Islamic architecture walking tours and learnt about the mosque of Ibn Tulun which dated from 876–879, was Mesopotamian in design and unique in

Cairo, the best-preserved of its kind in the world. Next door was the Gayer-Anderson house, an old-style residence which had been turned into a museum. 'In each house there is a reception room downstairs with balconies enclosed in mashrabiyya screens where the ladies of the harem could sit and watch the men.'

There was Old Cairo to explore, with its synagogue with beautiful stained-glass windows, and an old Coptic church. At the mosque, you could put on strange cotton covers for your shoes, like floppy tissue-box covers.

A photo of her at a party in Cairo shows Mum looking slim and elegant in a black dress with coral, white and green flowers. Straps at the shoulders. Her hair is a neat, glossy bob, she is tanned and her nails are painted. She's holding a glass. She must have liked this photo as it was one of a few in a small photo album in her house.

In typical corporate fashion, the first inkling of being moved again was through friends, contractors. 'I hear you're going,' a woman said to Mum. Mum asked her to ask the source of the gossip at bridge and at the same time, told me: 'I'm making my last-minute purchases just in case': she had some old copper jelly moulds lined with tin, and some spoons re-plated for 50 piastres each. She had brass bowls silver-plated for serving nuts and at dinner parties ('I'm keeping quiet about the idea of having brass silver-plated as someone like Nellwyn will rush down and have enormous quantities done and send the prices rocketing').

Sure enough, after they'd been in Egypt for three years, Dad visited head office in the States and the company told him they'd like him to see out the summer in Egypt, then move to Houston.

They spent a short time back home in Kent before heading off to the States. Dad went for a few weeks first. Mum and Fiona would go with him later. I was still in London. I'd only survived a year at Guy's Hospital Medical School (that's another story entirely), had worked for a year in London, and was starting law at Kings College, London. Fiona had left school and was going to do a secretarial course in Houston.

Dad stayed in what he called an 'apartment thing', known as a condominium over there. 'Anyway, it means a flat in a compound.' This one was part of a complex of forty units, or boxes, as Dad described them. People seemed thin on the ground, and he only saw one person 'scamper' from car to condo, in the first weekend there. When he went for a thirty-minute walk around a few blocks, he was the only person on the street. 'The stores are quite different from our shopping streets,' he reported: 'more like car parks with shops attached.' The 'country' he described as fairly wooded but 'flat, flat, flat. The flatness and the long straight roads are quite amazing.'

He went to look at the house he and Mum would rent. There were lots of details that were not to their taste: a 'loud' featured fireplace and chimney, built-in cupboards and shelves in the living room that he described as 'grot', bright yellow worktops in the kitchen. 'Anyway, it's not so bad and will look much different with our stuff in it!!'

A shipment would follow to Baltimore and they had packed a foot locker that was air freighted from Cairo, but they took what they could on the plane: five suitcases, one bike, three pieces of hand luggage and three coats. Arriving in Houston was quite something.

Once at their accommodation, they dumped the suitcases and paid a visit to the local supermarket, feeling very strange shopping at what would have been 2 am in England.

The first few days they spent in the condominium with access to a pool, jacuzzi (not partaken of) and tennis courts. Mum said she looked forward to moving to a house as 'everything is very limited here.' The kitchen had a large oven, microwave, dishwasher and garbage disposal unit, but no serving dishes; the laundry had a big family washing machine and dryer, but no iron or vacuum cleaner. The television, however, had thirteen channels, with a selection of films to watch in the evening. 'I go to bed first and read,' wrote Mum. 'The television is on so much, with Fiona during the day, that by 8.30 I've had more than enough noise!'

Mum had always had a soft spot for cats and one soon adopted them. It came in first thing every morning and stayed until they put him out at dinner time: a small tabby with half a tail. He seemed well fed, so they thought he had a home. But when he started to spend almost all day in the flat, they concluded he must be a stray. 'I don't feed him, just the odd scrap and bowl of milk. He's very sweet, his only bad point is that every time someone goes into the kitchen he rushes after them and screeches for food.'

Before moving into the house, Dad went to Chicago for a week. Mum had the car all week and busied herself setting up a new bank account, arranging a wiring of money from England, arranging for phone connection to the house, getting a certified cheque for a second car they were buying as it was difficult to get around otherwise.

The furniture arrived in Houston and would be delivered at 8 am one morning. Then there was the unpacking, washing every single plate, dish, knife, fork while setting up the kitchen; tracking down adaptors for lamps and electrical appliances. They lived in a faceless suburb with wide streets and smooth lawns front and back of large, bland houses. It was miles to anywhere.

Soon after arriving, Mum described to me the layout of Houston. 'Down town' was just like London 'down town', she said, with big offices and big stores. 'We've only been down there once—there's nothing to go there for really.' Then there were the suburbs, each with its big shopping mall with its car park and large stores. They lived in the north-east, the local shopping area had a supermarket, pharmacy, two 'dress shops', hardware shop, two hairdressers, dry-cleaners, bookshop, needlework shop, garden centre, gift shop, kitchen shop (expensive), snack bar, sports shop, two cinemas and a new McDonald's, Big-Burger, pizza shop and a chicken takeaway. Everything for your daily needs. For tools or Christmas decorations, you might need to go further afield to Humble (pronounced Umble), and for really big things, to Greenspoint, where Dad worked.

Letters continued to fly over the Atlantic in the company pouch. Please buy a *Harpers & Queen*, Mum asked me, and send the advertisements for houses and flats in London as some people she'd met wanted to buy a flat to let. Either a *Country Life* or *Harpers*; 'They are prepared to spend quite a bit of money. £2 enclosed.'

There were detailed descriptions of their efforts to buy a string of pearls for my twenty-first birthday. With instructions to look in England and the airport, to compare prices. 'We don't want you to have any rubbish. There's nothing nicer or more wearable than a good string of pearls but equally there's nothing worse than bad pearls.'

Soon after arriving, it was Thanksgiving, so Dad had a couple of days off. They went to San Antonio, 'about 200 miles west and is where the battle of the Alamo was. It is very Spanish in influence, with old Spanish missions ... It means leaving the house in a mess but we would have Saturday and Sunday to sort out the beds etc and then all the time in the world to get straight. It would be a nice little break after the four weeks here.' They stayed in the Hilton, on the River Walk—a great spot for evening strolls.

Mum investigated the local supermarket, checking every single row, to see what they stocked—then sent requests to me for a tin of custard powder and a bottle of mushroom ketchup (which she used along with Worcestershire sauce to make stock instead of using stock cubes). In another letter, a request for two tins of mustard—the dried English variety, to make French dressing.

Later on, she found another supermarket with a small 'foreign foods' section. Here she found Tiptree jams, Bath Oliver biscuits and Bisto gravy mix. It wasn't so much that they 'needed' or missed these, but she was interested to see what they had, and it would have seemed funny that these run-of-the-mill grocery items were displayed as foreign delicacies.

The pattern their lives took must be one repeated still by couples shifted around the globe with companies. The one with the job, in this case, my father, has work to focus on; the other, like my mother, has to find ways to, at best, stay fulfilled, at worst, fill the time. 'The big news of the week is that I've bought a piano,' she wrote one day. She'd seen one advertised in the suburb, just the other side of the lights. It was a small mahogany one, 'just what I wanted.'

A few months later she was having a weekly piano lesson. It was supposed to be a half-hour session, but usually went on for an hour as she was the last pupil of the day. She played for around two hours each day, 'but not all at once as my back starts aching!' After four lessons she reckoned she was probably back to her old standard already, with the teacher pushing her on to new things.

She took Spanish lessons for a while. It was a big class, about thirty people. 'I don't think we'll lose very many as the weeks go on ... the majority are quite intelligent types who shouldn't have much difficulty in keeping up. It's a nice sounding language and is similar to French in some ways.'

Houston must have seemed dull after Cairo, where just stepping out of the door was bound to be interesting. But Mum took up offers of outings when she could. She went to a herb farm at Cleveland, but wasn't impressed at the way there were tiny herb patches scattered about among weeds.

'I've never seen such a mess in my life!' nor was she impressed with the cold lunch which took three hours to serve. But she did buy fresh herbs to pot up at home: mint, chives, oregano, thyme and basil—that she later reported were 'growing like mad.'

She wrote telling me of what sounded to me—and no doubt were for her—incongruous outings, like the time they went with company friends to a Renaissance festival about 50 miles north of Houston. The place was set up like an old English village and people were dressed in medieval costume 'of sorts'. There was jousting, plays, strolling minstrels and each 'house' was a stall selling various things from Western hats to hot dogs. Another weekend they were invited for a barbecue where the chickens were scorched till they were black, and the hostess talked non-stop for at least two hours. I can just imagine Mum cringing inside at these clumsy shows of culture.

They set out to a flea market near the city, 'but it was just new junk'; they drove through Splendora heading north, to see what it was like, 'but it wasn't very splendid! In fact when you get out of the "smart" areas it is pretty rough—very poor looking "shack" houses with gardens full of junk.'

It was all a far cry from Cairo. Dad wrote, 'As you will see when you get here, there are not all that many places to see—no castles, no mosques, no chateaus!

Anyway, it's different and their sights are unusual. Even the roads are unusual.'

They found it very strange and different compared to Europe: 'There are run down, tumble down places which are rough, rough, rough. Then there are the ultra modern, almost film screen sets.' The suburb they lived in fitted that category, Dad said. 'There are lots of so called trailer parks. We would call them caravan settlements. Not quite gipsy, but in some places so. They excel in shops, eating places, roads and cars! Also expensive fun.'

Cars dominated. And they came in large size only, more or less. Once, when Mum walked to the hairdressers, perhaps a twenty-minute walk, the staff could barely believe she'd got there by foot. It seemed eccentric to them. The freeways were a thick stream of cars. On the sides were the brash neon signs, up on sticks like cocktail snacks, advertising restaurants. It seemed unbelievably tasteless.

But what they lost in ancient culture and chaos, they gained in ease. 'Supermarket shopping is so easy here. You just wheel your trolley to the checkout, the front of the trolley folds down, so the girl can take out the things, someone puts them in bags for you and puts them on your trolley and will wheel it out to your car and put it in the boot!'

The whole process was so quick. The new-to-her barcode system impressed: 'The checkout assistant doesn't have to keep pressing buttons on a till all the time.' So too the fact that you could buy stamps at the supermarket. In fact, she was quite tickled at the whole efficiency of the mail system: 'If I want to post a letter I put the right amount of stamps on it, put it in my mail box outside, put the red flag on the mail box up and the post lady takes it. Good, isn't it?'

They did their best to make the most of being there, but it wasn't a happy household. They usually went out and about at the weekend, but the weekdays could drag. Fiona missed England and her friends. When Dad left for work, Mum was asleep. By the time he came back from work she was tipsy. Cairo had been busy, filled with the company of acquaintances, if not close friends, and there was plenty to occupy the mind. In Cairo, you could join in the expat community life and maybe feel a little special, a little privileged for it; in Houston, you were just another executive family. She wasn't one to ever talk about whether she was bored, or lonely, or unhappy. You had to read her by what she was doing and how she was acting. With absorbing projects, she was good. I tend to think that it was in Egypt, with all the parties and entertaining, that she would have 'discovered' alcohol and perhaps developed a taste for it. Certainly, it wasn't a problem before then that I could remember. But in Houston, it must have become an escape.

I'd gone to Egypt at every opportunity and loved it, but I only visited Houston twice. The atmosphere in the house was pretty bad, I disliked where they lived and the whole place had little charm for me. Mum used to stay up late after Dad had gone to bed, listening to melancholic music.

On one of my trips one Christmas—I think my grandparents were visiting too—we went to the Tumbleweed, a place where they played country music and served obscene-sized steaks with potatoes (or chips) and coleslaw. We danced. Mum laughed and danced, was bubbly on wine. She wobbled and giggled but we didn't find it funny. It's the only time I can remember her letting go with alcohol—I wish we could have just seen the funny side. It probably didn't help that we all watched her like a hawk. Looking for the changes of expression ... signs that she'd slipped a glass too many.

Usually they explored at weekends, driving to places like Galveston, a day trip away. Compared to much of Houston, it seemed to have character and be easy on the English eye. They went to Corpus Christi near the Mexican border and, with friends they used to know in Cairo, to Cancun, a small island off the Yucatán peninsula, on the 'toe' of Mexico. The beachside hotel reminded them of Egypt: slow service, leaking ceiling in the bedroom—although, unlike Egypt, they said, it was clean. Mum used to enjoy these sorts of trips. They saw Mayan ruins at Tulum; a lagoon called Xel-la (pronounced, wrote Mum, 'shell-la'); more ruins at Chichen Itza ('Cheatsen eatsa'). Many of the buildings were for ceremonial purposes, she told me, ever the keen cultural tourist. They climbed all 192 steps of the pyramid-like temple. 'They were really steep and my legs ached for days!' They passed through quite a few modern Mayan villages, with their thatched-roofed houses that had wooden poles for walls. Although the houses didn't have windows, the doors were often open and Mum could see inside:

> They just have a dirt floor with hammocks as beds and usually just a table and chairs. But some have televisions and fridges. They farm in the rainy season—May to Sept but only grow corn, beans and squash as the ground is limestone with just a few feet of soil on top. Then in the dry season they hunt. There were lots of pigs, turkeys, chickens running around and the occasional cow. They are Christian but also pray to the rain God! Very sensible I think.

They returned from their Mexican trip on Thanksgiving Day and found to their 'horror and amazement' that all the shops were closed, even McDonald's. Fiona hadn't gone on the trip, nor had she got any food in, and the only thing they could find nearby was a cheap and nasty hotel meal.

Local entertainment included rodeos. 'On Sunday we went to the Texas prison rodeo. It's exactly as it sounds—a rodeo in a prison and the competitors are the prisoners!' That particular one was supposed to be rougher than usual because the prisoners weren't professionals and took more risks. Everyone—except them—wore jeans, boots and stetson hats. They really enjoyed the experience, although they weren't too impressed with the 'star' at half-time, a writer called Tom J. Hall: 'We didn't think much of him, but the crowd loved him.'

They'd go and see the tennis finals in the Astrodome complex, the Virginia Slims or World Championships—hoping to see Chris Evert or Jimmy Connors.

They explored downtown Houston, as the centre was known. Mum told me in detail once about a hunt for sandals. She found they were either poor quality or expensive Italian ones, but in the end found some red slingbacked, peep-toe shoes which would do. While waiting to meet Dad at the end of the day, she and Fiona studied passers-by. 'The shoe standard is poor generally—people were wearing either tennis shoes or the sandals with big rubber wedges that I'd rejected.'

Prices were similar to back home in England, she decided, especially with the pound so low. But eating out was cheap.

One of the things I remember clearly about my visits to Houston was the weather. Over the span of a few days around Christmas we had both snow, and a day hot enough to sunbathe.

It was often hot and humid: 'This week has been revolting—it's so humid (97.5%) and about 85 with thick grey cloudy skies.' Sometimes the temperature swung wildly and there were flood and tornado warnings. Whenever it was nice, Mum would sit outside. She bought loungers for the garden so they could stretch out on warm days.

There was a nest in the honeysuckle near the gate at the house. When the eggs hatched, Mum would peer into it when the mother bird was away. There were three babies, she reported, who squawked all the time, audible even in the kitchen with the radio on. 'The poor bird works all day long getting food.'

They bought a hummingbird feeder which was used nearly non-stop by two hummingbirds. 'You make up a sugar and water syrup and put red food colouring in it so they can spot it easily,' said Mum. Since the feeder had a little perch around it, the birds stayed a while.

At Christmas, Mum put a wreath on the front door and a twig basket full of fir cones and red apples for the hall chest. One neighbour had a 'block party'—for everyone in the block. They laughed at the oversize Christmas decorations that were put up on the neighbourhood lawns and roofs: Bambi, Snoopy, Santa Claus and a life-size nativity scene.

Dad travelled on business every now and then, back to Cairo a few times and to Chicago. Mum joined him one Friday in Chicago after he'd been there for a week-long course. She left Houston on a 92-degree Friday morning and arrived, after a delayed flight, to a cool and rainy Chicago of 60 degrees. They bought two umbrellas and set out from their centrally located hotel in their macs 'to go walkabout.' She wrote:

It's a 'proper' city with masses of shops and people
etc. We went to a ticket place like the one in Leicester
Square and got 1/2 price tickets for Evita that night.
Then we walked for miles looking for a 'fantastic'
pizza place Dad had been to. We found it and
ordered and he began to have doubts as to whether it
was the right place. We had undrinkable wine and
pizzas which were revolting! Then when we came out
and were walking down the street we passed the one
which he had meant us to be in!

But the show, at a new theatre that seated 5000, and with the Broadway cast, was 'very good', thankfully. The next morning they set off again to the Sears Tower, then the world's tallest building, took a boat trip around the lakeshore and river and went to a 'nice' restaurant in the evening for dinner. On Sunday morning they checked out of the hotel, left the bags there and walked down to the lakeshore and on to the aquarium, then after lunch in a hotel, flew back. Reading back over her description of this trip, I was impressed at how they packed their time. She obviously enjoyed the city and thought it superior to Houston.

She'd go back to England a couple of times a year, oversee the cutting of the hay in the big field, or work they had done on the house. Once, she even spotted a house that she toyed with the idea of buying. Mum had always wanted a period home, a house hundreds of years old, creaking with character. She liked a house that came up in the area, but Dad didn't want to leave their own. He felt attached to it and the land, and to purchase a house while living overseas and not come back to the one they left would be unbearable, he said. No sale.

Mum was back in England for a break once, and after one phone call in particular I became very worried about her drinking. She'd sounded very slurred. I was very concerned and spoke to Dad about it. I was still living in London. I went to an Al-Anon meeting or two, the offshoot of Alcoholics Anonymous for the friends and relatives of people with drinking problems. People talked of their parents, or whoever, hiding bottles of whisky in airing cupboards or under the bed, of loud scenes and far, far worse things than anything Mum ever got up to. The philosophy was that you couldn't influence them, and that one day, they'd have to pick themselves up, and every time you put all the pieces back together again for them, they were another step away from facing the problem themselves. Don't watch, they said, don't count the drinks. It was a healthy attitude, I thought, though I wondered how you'd put it into practice if you were living the everyday with an alcoholic. It was my father who bore the brunt of her destructive practice. I, now living away from home, was fairly sheltered from it, although Mum treated me like a stranger for several months after Dad told her I was concerned. I took what I could from the Al-Anon meetings, but two was enough. I didn't really need to hug strangers once a week.

When the time came to leave Houston, no one was sorry. Fiona had survived her stay and had secretarial skills she could now use to find work in England; Dad would get back to his fields and horses; Mum would be back in her own house again.

FIVE

PICKING UP THE PIECES

It was so so wonderful to be coming back home to my family in Australia. I was glad to have gone back to England for my mother, and even to have enjoyed the old churches and pubs around the villages where I grew up. But it was here, with my husband and two boys, that I belonged.

I arrived back in Sydney in the morning. Peter was to take Harry to school, accompanied by Felix. I'd been back in the house a little while and there was a knock and some voices at the door. 'Is Mummy back yet?' I heard Peter saying. Felix's face grinned widely as I opened up. He looked so small!

The place hadn't been as bad as I'd been led to expect. There were three bunches of flowers and a big banner on the floor saying 'Welcome Home Alison'. There was coffee ready to go and champagne in the fridge. Peter had been counting the days, I knew. And even the hours in the last few days. I was surprised to be able to see the floors—and to see that they were quite clean. It turned out that since our 'God has vomited ... ' conversation he'd had a last-minute burst of energy and activity and decided to tidy up a bit. What he'd done, I realised a little later, was simply to pile anything and everything that was on the floor or chairs—or other places they shouldn't be—onto surfaces like the top of a cupboard or a chest of drawers. It took me months to sort through the archaeology of layers he'd created in my two weeks' absence.

But it was just so good to be back I didn't care. Mess, moaning ... I didn't care about it. It was life. I wanted life now. No more choosing headstones or feeling I was creeping about in someone else's house ... My home. My life. It was wonderful. I felt almost melted with relaxation. Things had a sensuous quality about them. I was seeing things with new eyes—colours, light, the feeling of a sexy hug. Life—let me back in!

I went with Peter later on in the day to pick up Harry from school. On seeing me he ran down the hill from his classroom and jumped to me with a flashing smile. Harry seemed to have grown in the fortnight I had been away, and one of his new teeth had moved down into his mouth.

Well ... they had survived! It turned out they'd run almost every day to school and everyone who'd seen Peter during the time I was away said he seemed very rushed and busy and counting the days till I returned. Harry had missed a couple of days of school here and there but Peter hadn't had to resort to taking Felix extra days to day care. Violin practice had fallen by the wayside but they were fed and clothed. Every nail on their bodies, I couldn't help noticing, needed cutting, however!

I had a strong sense of a new start; getting back to my life: the children, my work, the house and friends. Sad events had been faced and sad tasks undertaken, but they were behind me now. In England, someone had said to me, referring to dealing with Mum's death and her funeral and house, that it would be the hardest thing I'd do in my life. While it was sad and I wished her life hadn't quite turned out the way it did, at least there was a sense of a daughter seeing her mother die as being in the right order. To bury a child would be much harder. I felt that if burying a sixty-year-old mother was the worst I'd experience, I'd be getting off pretty lightly. It doesn't take much imagination to conceive of far harder tasks. There was a new mother at the school that I'd met briefly in the week or so before going back to England. On my return, she asked how it had been. I mentioned these thoughts and she responded, 'It's so good to hear you say that. I lost a baby in a miscarriage a few years ago and it was dreadful. I remember thinking that it would be easier to lose my mother than lose this baby.'

Harry had been promised a kitten. And now that I was back, there was no excuse. He'd actually been promised one when we went to England but once it seemed unlikely that we'd be staying longer than a year we had to reconsider. He was then five and desperate for a pet, but I explained that it wouldn't really be fair to get a kitten and only a matter of months later have to find it another home. How would he feel about getting goldfish instead of a kitten? I'd asked him, sitting in the sunny summery garden in Yeoford.

'Don't fish mind changing owners?' he asked.

'They've got poor eyesight,' I told him. 'They can't really see who it is feeding them, so they don't mind as long as they get fed.'

He nodded and processed the information. He didn't seem convinced. 'When would I be able to get a goldfish?' he asked.

I shrugged my shoulders. 'Tomorrow?'

'YAY!!' he shouted with an arm thrust into the air. Kitten out, goldfish in. Sure enough we'd made a goldfish shopping trip the next day: two fish, one plain old goldfish and one with a fluttery, flashy tail; a tank, some weed, a couple of snails and some food. He'd got medium pleasure out of the fish and a vague fascination when one died—I found it floating on top of the water. We buried it in the garden and Harry made a little cardboard cross. It was the one with the fancy tail. He was soon replaced but his replacement met a sticky end too. I'd found him floating with a piece of gravel in his mouth. Fish suicide? It certainly looked like it. But apparently it is quite a common death in the goldfish world. They suck gravel for the algae—and every now and then they choke.

In the days after hearing of Mum's death and leaving for the UK, we'd talked of getting a kitten again, and I promised we'd get one when I returned. It was something for us all to look forward to.

The days rolled on and it was soon Harry's birthday. I had a plan. I'd called the RSPCA but there were no kittens available. Had I left it too late? I thought there were always some cute fluffy bundles wanting a home. But no. The lady on the phone told me, however, about an internet site called Catmatch. I logged on and there were a few lines about a 'short-haired domestic' at a vet in Paddington. I called them. There had been two but now there was only one left. He wasn't short-haired, he was long-haired. Black with some white markings. Blue eyes. He'd had his shots and a microchip and was ready to go. The idea was to surprise Harry and pick up a kitten after school. So this was it. Could they keep him till tomorrow afternoon? I definitely wanted it. He would be a birthday present for a seven-year-old boy. So it was really important they kept him. 'Yes ... fine, fine.'

I wrote out an 'Exceedingly important ticket' for Harry's birthday. And after school we jumped in a taxi and set off for the vet. There was the little kitten. In a large cage on the reception desk.

'Are there any others?' Harry asked. He liked the idea of choosing one from a litter.

'No, this is the only one left.'

'Okay then.' We paid up and put him in a special cardboard box shaped like a house with the roof for handles. He meowed all the way home in the taxi.

We talked about names. 'Blackie,' suggested Harry.

'Why don't you come up with a few names tonight or over the next few days and choose one later,' I countered, thinking we could do better than that. Besides, my family had already had a cat called Blackie. A farm cat that had been abandoned when his owners moved. He had been used to a little company and treats like broken eggs and was forlorn when left alone. He'd wandered up to my parents' house and they'd given him scraps of food outside. His coat was dull and he seemed slow on the uptake. Eventually he came in. Adopted. With a little care and a warm place to sleep at night he picked up. His coat regained its gloss; he even started to play. It was obvious. He'd been depressed!

For our new family member, I liked the idea of a link with my mother. I liked the name Oscar, as she'd died on Oscar Wilde's birthday, had some of his lines on her gravestone and had admired his writing. I also liked the idea that as my mother was spending her last days, unbeknownst to her, this little black bundle came into the world and began his life.

We had other names on the list but Harry liked 'Oscar' too—although I think he quickly forgot one, that it was me who'd thought of the name, and two, why I'd liked it. So Oscar it was.

The images and memories I had of Mum were at first dominated by her time at Burwash. Of course, that was the most recent, so it's not such a surprise. But sometimes I'd wanted to push my mind back further. I felt like she occupied a massive part of my brain and my make-up. But I didn't seem to be able to access much of it. A few images slipped out. But many were not good. I tried to think of times in my childhood when she had been kind. I remembered Mum comforting me as a small child. I was upset I hadn't woken up to say goodbye to my father. I remember a feeling of shame. Was he just going to work as normal or was he going on a trip? Why was it such a big deal? My memory fails me again.

In other snapshots she is telling me I'm as big as a house. We're in a restaurant with our French exchange guests. I'm being served peas and don't say 'stop' soon enough. I was around fifteen and we all counted calories at school and weighed ourselves each morning. I weighed 8 stone 10 pounds. A healthy teenager.

There were times after Dad had left her, before she moved out of the house and before she became ill, that we'd talk and I'd ask something out of bounds. Down came the curtains. 'Good night, Alison,' she'd dismiss me, tightening the fold of her arms and closing her face.

But the equilibrium was restored in a funny way during her last six or so years. We all agreed that somehow she'd 'come good'. We made more effort for her. As if her crisis exposed her vulnerability. She needed us—she made it clear that she needed and loved us, in her own, sometimes brittle, sometimes sentimental, way (particularly as the sun disappeared behind the rooftops and a glass or two of wine had disappeared too). We rallied round with regular phone calls, letters, extra tolerance, biting our tongues, forgiving her misplaced snobbery ... birthdays and Christmas calls always remembered.

'You won't recognise her,' my aunt Sheila warned me on my first visit after her 'crash'. I was visiting with one-year-old Harry. I'd been fed descriptions of my mother from various visitors. My friend Rachel had visited her in hospital, taken her flowers and told me how frail she looked. She'd always been thin. Now we approached 'wasted'. But there was puffiness too. Puffy face. Padding the bones, swollen flesh over her waist, legs ...

She spent a month in hospital, including her fifty-fourth birthday. When she was finally discharged she set herself the challenge of climbing her stairs to the first floor, to the bathroom and bedroom. She had to have railings fitted on the stairs and a great elaborate setup in the bath. The kitchen was rearranged so an oven was at waist height—so there'd be a chance of her having the strength to lift a pot out. She hated the adjustments—they looked ugly, she said. But it was that or a nursing home. She fought that idea. Good on her. A home help was arranged. She'd help with housework and also with baths and hair washes, which

Mum could not do alone. She was officially disabled. She got a sticker for her car and a walking stick. She was fifty-four ... fifty-four! When I think back to that I'm still amazed. Peter turned fifty-four a few years ago. I get annoyed when he resists change and sometimes feel the thirteen years between us. But when he was fifty-four he pulled Felix on his extender bike up the hills, he walked any distance, loved a party and still does. A world removed.

Once Mum had settled down a bit and we got to know her limits, I learnt a way of dealing with her, albeit at a long arm's length since I lived in Australia. Don't call before 10 am because she's nauseous first thing, till she's had her pills. (We all heard the story of how to keep the first ones down. Was it a cracker and a glass of water? or a minuscule slice of fruit cake?) I would not call in the later afternoon/evening either, as you could never be sure what state she'd be in. When we visited on holiday, too. I tended to suggest lunchtimes and avoided staying overnight. It was easier just to set the boundary.

It was hot back in Australia. I had a book to write, and emails still flowed between Fiona and me concerning Mum: how the clearing of her house had gone, and what had been fetched at auction; the pricing of her headstone and other matters. Another part of the mix, however, was correspondence from her solicitor. As I commented on the snowfall in Tunbridge Wells that I'd heard about on the news or radio, and how my boys would have loved it, was it appropriate to add it was so hot here in Sydney that I was down to my underwear while sitting at the keyboard? Definitely not!

Christmas approached. We put the Christmas tree up one morning. We had bought it the previous day. It was such a hot day, the girl at the grocery shop suggested we hose it before bringing it in. So the tree got a hosing—much to the delight of two small boys—and stayed outside for the night. We brought it in the next morning and stood it up in the corner of our dining room by the big mirror, in the new Christmas tree stand. Something moved at the top. It was a tiny lizard! A Christmas lizard instead of a fairy, we laughed.

I got teary unwrapping the old glass baubles I'd taken from the cellar at Mum's house and brought home in my suitcase. Fiona had chosen the tacky decorations—gaudy elves and fat Father Christmases. I liked the ones we'd had as children: frosted bells, stars made of silvery beads, shimmering balls of pale blue and yellow. They seemed so beautiful and delicate. They still were but I was surprised at how tarnished some were too: faded ribbons on a string of silver balls, with a patina of rust. I still liked them though, despite, probably because of, the way they wore over the years.

I remembered one year asking Mum for a Christmas decoration and she said she liked the idea of something she'd had for years being used on our Christmas trees in years to come. So I liked the idea now that if Mum could know, she'd like it that we put up the snowman with wings and little wall hangings of a boy angel and Father Christmas. It made me think too of the year she wrote to me telling me that she'd put up Christmas decorations in celebration of being alive. Christmas was a hard time for her in the later years but it was a sign of strength that she celebrated it, and a sign that she'd chosen life.

My little shipment arrived from England a few weeks into the New Year. When it arrived, it formed a mound in the dining room of large items wrapped in brown paper and tape. The antique gold velvet winged chair; a small old pine box that Mum had had in her sitting room and used to store videos, now stuffed with items; another wicker box that had been in the bathroom; a log basket. A couple of blankets, the coat, a few books and jumpers, a couple of shirts. Is this all? I couldn't help thinking. It seemed such a pathetic pile, all that remained to me of someone's life. The thought niggled me that I should have taken more things. But I had such a long way to bring them, little space to store anything … and it didn't really matter, I knew that. 'You let go after a while,' my friend Lesley had said, who'd lost her mother as a young medical student. I kept thinking of Mum's house full to the brim of lovely things and in the end, as an exercise, made myself write down the items I wished I'd had. It came down to a walnut blanket box, a beautifully made piece of furniture she kept on her upstairs landing, with a large circular grain and deep warm golden colour; an antique pine wardrobe—that wouldn't even fit in our house, so that was easy to dismiss; and a few silver photo frames. I felt I should have taken those frames because they were 'good' and 'nice', but at the same time, I knew why I hadn't. They were showy and I didn't like the images in them: one of them, the only one of me in the house, in my graduating gear (the only photo I have of me in it and it's hideous), with my eyes just beginning to close. (Moral—if you are lucky enough to dress up in gowns for a graduation ceremony, ask someone to take some informal shots too.) Another one seemed to me to be like a trophy of her marriage, her and Dad patting a horse. Once I'd itemised those things, it was easy to see it wasn't a big deal and I could live with my choices.

✤

Still, knowing Mum's house was now empty and her belongings scattered was a strange feeling. Out of the blue I'd sometimes think of some thing and wonder what had happened to it. A friend's dream told me I wasn't the only one thinking over the things that had been bound into my mother's life. She'd dreamt her father was back in the house, in bed, looking terrible. He hadn't died after all, but looked a wreck. He'd gathered all the battered bits of furniture that had scattered among family—a table, a chair. 'It was just pathetic,' she said.

One of the things I kept thinking about was the handbag Mum had been using, and her purse. And although Dad had restrained much of his curiosity about the destiny of many of her belongings—which they'd mostly shared at some point in their life—he did mention a large black horse with an Asian look that had sat in the inglenook fireplace. 'Fiona's having that,' he'd said. When I'd mentioned it to Fiona she hadn't realised it meant much to him but now felt obliged to take it rather than sell it with everything else. What had happened to it? Had she kept it after all?

I sent Fiona an email asking about these few items which had been bugging me.

'Yes, I have the handbag and yes I have the purse and yes I have the horse!!!!' Fiona emailed me back. 'The black horse sits in the entrance hall here with my old pink teddy bear riding him and an occasional cap or hat!'

'Yesterday must have been a "Mum" day,' she continued. 'I had a phone call from school saying that Hope had got very upset on two occasions reading a book which was on the curriculum and she refused to say what it was about and couldn't stop crying.'

It turned out the story was about a great-aunt who lived upstairs in her house and had friends bring her shopping and do her favours. The character had reminded Hope of her grandmother, Mum.

Later in the year Peter was in Devon and he called on Fiona and she gave him my mother's purse as well as a couple more recipe scrapbooks. The handbag was still in the boot of her car where she'd put it when she first removed it from Cygnet Cottage.

It was funny receiving the purse. It is a nice quality, soft navy leather, just beginning to get a worn look. One tiny tear along the edge of one pocket and a couple of wrinkles. It is smooth to the touch and pleasant to rub my fully stretched fingers on it. It is of the folding type, opening out like a wallet, with many pockets.

I still have it in the drawer of my desk where I must have been sitting when Peter produced it out of his suitcase. Fiona and I had spent the money inside it, but nothing else was removed except a couple of passport photographs of her in her younger, snappier days.

Here is what's inside it still:

Back pocket—the business card of Bridget Todd, manager of Bell House Fabrics, Cranbrook, with Mum's phone number written in a wobbly version of her own handwriting, plus her postcode; A Marks & Spencer card with a Personal Customer Reference Number.

The front layer works like a purse. Inside—in one pocket, pink strips of receipt paper from Pipers News Store dated a month or so before she died; and a finger-sized swatch of dusky pink fabric. I recognise it as matching the material backing some of her tapestry cushions.

In the bigger central pocket—a brass key; twenty-one British Isles postage stamps of various denominations and colours: blue, green, orange and brown. She used to remove stamps that hadn't been franked and would send the Australian ones back to me to use again.

More funny pink receipt strips, the last one dated 05/10/02 (nine days before she died), for £1.85.

A little magazine cutting about St Michael Tuscan Extra Virgin olive oil, given a Good Food Best Buy. Another small cutting about Fior D'Olio Extra Virgin Puglia, with a Good Food Equal Favourite.

A recorded mail sticker stamped 19.Mar.97. That's a long

time to keep a recorded mail receipt! Whatever it was was sent to Circus House, Brighton. Is it a coincidence that the date is my father's birthday? What was she up to then? It was after their separation and after her health crisis, I work out.

There's a strange piece of cardboard with a large black H printed on a yellow background and what looks like serial numbers of a piece of home electrics or some such.

Some address labels: Mrs E Haynes, Cygnet Cottage .... with British Heart logos on them.

Some Co-op vouchers: £1 off Findus Feeling Great Range (350 g) and £1 off Energizer E2 Titanium Battery Range, plus 25p off Co-op Unsmoked Rindless Back Bacon or Co-op Scottish Unsmoked Rindless Bacon 250/500 g.

And a few more receipts.

In the back layer of the purse, in the slits where credit cards can go—a white strip of paper with the words,

'Bachelor of English and French Law (LLB)

Maitrise de Droit Privé (Master of Private Law)'.

These are my qualifications! To think she carried that around in her purse! Just in case she wanted to drop it into a conversation? It makes me smile, chuckle a bit even now. But I'm touched, too, that she was so proud—maybe even impressed.

An NHS card, filled in with her NHS number, address and doctor's contact details.

In a wider pocket—three slim yellow cards which appear to be library reservation cards. 'Fee paid for purchase of this card is not refundable' it says on the back. 'A further charge will be payable when the reserved item is collected.' The books being requested are: *Jane and May Morris, 1839–1938*, by Jan Marsh; *The Clarice Cliff Colour Price Guide*, by H. & P. Watson; and *Collecting Decanters*, by Jane Hollingsworth.

Another NHS document; this one is a Certificate of Prepayment of Charges, for £31.90. Among the notes on the back it states that the certificate covers NHS charges for drugs, appliances and elastic hosiery ... It does not (in bold) cover NHS wigs and fabric supports.

A driving licence, still with its printout 'Your New Driving Licence'. It is signed with Mum's straightforward signature—no more than her normal handwriting—and has her Burwash address. But there's no date of issue. It is simply valid from 24 01 1977 to 09 08 2012—the day before what would have been her seventieth birthday.

In the last pocket furthest back—another key, a clunky brass one; a Sentinel Helpline Card with her name, policy number, blood type (A positive, like me) and allergies (Septrin). I didn't know she was allergic to anything. There's her doctor's phone number, but nothing entered for next of kin.

A large handwritten receipt on white paper, headed in

a stylish black typeface, with pale blue lines where it is filled in. It is from Charles Moss Ltd, Craftsmen Furriers, 118–120 High Street, Esher, Surrey. It is dated 19.9.85. It is almost twenty years old. It's made out in florid, slightly out-of-control handwriting to Mrs Haynes, Hawkhurst. One Female Stranded Natural Ranel Mink Coat. £2800 less deposit £280. Balance £2520. At the bottom, the small print asks, 'Would customers please note that we do not accept liability for loss or damage to customers' furs while they are in our possession or with our processors.'

What happened to her wretched mink coat? I didn't want it. Fiona didn't want it. Nor did Sheila or Máire. Yet she'd almost shimmered and shivered with pride when she got it. It always seemed a bit over-the-top to me. I guess that pride and joy went to Help the Aged and someone got a bargain. It hadn't aged as such—she looked after her things.

Flattened next to the fur receipt, a couple more coupons: 20p off Pine Fresh Flash Liquid. 'Please don't embarrass your retailer by asking him to accept this coupon against any item other than Flash Liquid.' And 30p Coupon Towards Your Next Purchase of Sun Powder, Sun Liquid or Sun Rinse Aid.

And finally, three empty library cards which appear to have expired a year before Mum died. Maybe they weren't too fussy about dates.

It must seem odd in some ways to have delved into my mother's purse so intently, and then to have almost obsessively listed its contents. Of course, it is a very personal item, used every day, and for that it retains a specialness for me. At some level, there is childish curiosity about what your mother's purse or handbag contains, especially if she (unlike me, who swaps from week to week) maintains the sole, almost sacred one that follows her everywhere. I would like to think I am beyond that stage. For me, my mother's purse represents a life cut short. It is a snapshot of the many aspects of the life she was leading, up to the day she died. What does it reveal? An organised person, with enough time and will to cut out the money-saving coupons; I hesitate to use the word 'intellectual', but yes, there was an intellectual curiosity there, with the books she was hoping to collect soon and her strong interest in history.

There are the hints of her hobbies and interests: the card from the fabric shop; the swatch of material; again, the books on order. And pointers too to what was important to her. The pride in the receipt for the coat—perhaps a symbol to her of her success in life, that she'd married a man who'd done well and could, later on, afford such a luxury. (Even though she was now separated from him.) The slip of paper with my qualifications written on it: again, the flush of success, 'my daughter studied at the

Sorbonne.' (Even though the truth was that I'd hated law and had been really unhappy.)

There, too, the facts in black and white, about her health. The NHS documents, the Sentinel card, the rather sad lack of contact details entered for next of kin.

I found it a relief to discover these small demonstrations that my mother was leading a full, engaged life right to the end. She'd had disappointments. Her life had not taken the turns it might have. She almost gave up at some point. But here in this purse I see her little enthusiasms, a certain zest for life that I'm happy she had.

A friend told me she'd read one of the books Mum had on order, the one on Jane and May Morris, and what a fascinating book it was, about the wife and daughter of William Morris, designer and major founder of the British Arts and Crafts Movement. Both women's talents were overshadowed by William's fame. Would this aspect have been of interest to my mother? Quite possibly, as well as being interested in the movement (I had William Morris curtains in my bedroom at Ightham), she'd read several books about the wives of famous writers. One on Kipling's wife, Carrie, and another one, I vaguely remember, on Dylan Thomas's wife, Caitlin. Her last birthday present to me was a bundle of books, each about women: *Georgiana, Duchess of Devonshire; Daughters of Britannia, The lives and times of diplomatic wives;* and *Mrs Keppel and Her Daughter.* I wouldn't have said before that Mum had much interest in women's affairs as such; she was definitely not a feminist. After I was married it took me a long time to persuade her that I was not Mrs P. Needham, but Ms A. Haynes, as I had not changed my name after marrying. But perhaps she had a growing interest in women's lot in life. Once, when she'd said something about me doing Peter's ironing, and I'd replied, 'I don't do his ironing. We do our own,' she'd looked surprised but genuinely pleased. 'Good for you,' she said.

I turned forty the birthday after Mum died. She died in October, my birthday is in February. Before she died, I'd thought maybe I'd have a big party, maybe a bush dance. I'd got as far as thinking of possible halls, and wondering how I'd find a good band to play and call dances. But when my birthday came around, four months after she died, I wasn't in the mood for a big fuss. Four of us (two others who'd also just turned forty and Peter) went out for a beautiful French meal instead. At the time, I did think a little about what it meant to be forty. Was it any different to another birthday? Yes and no. I thought perhaps it was time to shake off expectations from others, but I can't say I made any major changes. Never one to shy away from reflection, I was also beginning to be aware that it was in her forties that Mum seemed to decline. I was certainly not planning that road.

When we returned to Australia after our year in England, we'd envisaged moving out of Sydney but still weren't quite sure about it. While away I'd made a mental note to explore the Illawarra, south of the Royal National Park just beyond Sydney's southern outskirts, but on our immediate return, we were involved in setting up house again and finding work. After Mum died we more or less decided not to make any decisions to move till a year had passed. While she was alive, I had felt a strong pull to the UK. In fact, once she'd been diagnosed with dilated cardiomyopathy, and had such a grim prognosis to begin with, it had entered my head that, had I been single, I would probably have gone back to England to live. But I wasn't single, and didn't feel I could uproot everyone willy-nilly. I had a responsibility to the people in my young family as well as my parental one. As Dad was much more mobile and could easily visit me if he wanted, when Mum died, the tie to England lessened significantly. It wasn't that I didn't like England, or was hooked on Australia even, just that Australia was where I was, our bread appeared to be buttered here, and things were pretty good. The place didn't seem to matter so much, I wasn't going to fritter away my life pining for another country.

Still, our terrace was small, to say the least. The children of some friends who lived in the country called it a dolls' house. We wanted to move, and Peter wanted a garden. But we weren't going to rush anywhere. I was aware that Mum's death would stir up all sorts of feelings about 'home' and we wanted any decision we made to be a good one.

So no immediate plans, we said, but nothing stopped us exploring ideas. Our minds were still open to the possibility of moving and on one trip to New Zealand to see his mother, a seed was planted in Peter's head. That seed was Dunedin. He—and perhaps I caught it too—became mildly obsessed with the possibility of moving to Dunedin in the South Island of New Zealand. Low crime rate, no earthquakes, good weather (neither of us, unlike many of our Sydney friends, mind a touch of cold), no mosquitoes, he reckoned, university town, so a bit of life about it. Real estate very, very reasonable. We looked up the seasonal highs and lows—temperatures were about the same as parts of Devon, where we'd been very happy temperature-wise, thank you very much. Flights to Sydney, a touch of culture, possibly—theatres, restaurants, art gallery ... the whole of the South Island to explore. Too remote? That was its appeal! In the post September 11 world, Peter liked the idea of being in the type of place he imagined no one considered part of world politics. Only trouble was I'd never been there in my life, and Peter had spent one day (two?) a good twenty years ago. I looked up information on the internet, we bought street maps of the city, we exchanged the odd email about a particular house, four bedrooms ... how much? Can it be true? Before we got too side-tracked we thought we should visit. The idea was taking over an unreasonably large part of the brain. We'd go for a South Island holiday—a selected 'we-have-children-and-don't-like-driving-hundreds-of-kilometres-a-day' holiday—and check out Dunedin at the same time.

It was a bit on/off for a while as the fluctuations in the bank balances of two freelance writers are a little wild for comfort sometimes. Looked like we could afford it, then a few bills to pay all at once and ... perhaps no.

'Have you got the money?' Peter would ask, knowing I wasn't exactly at peak earning capacity in my current situation.

'No.'

Then a modest sum in Mum's bank accounts was ready to release and Fiona and I were sent some money. It was quite a shock when one morning I picked up the phone for a spot of phone banking—checking the balance of my everyday account. It was significantly boosted. Not a bolt out of the blue, but it hit me. I rang to tell Peter—he had become financially sensitive since we had children and always appreciates knowing at least one of us has a little put away—and I started crying. I guess it was still only a matter of months since Mum had died. But I suppose what was different about this event was that this was the first sign, in a way, of her life affecting my life. Her life on this plane at least was over and up to now I had felt more in the role of—not mopping up, that's too mundane a word, but tying up the loose ends of her life, sealing it with the rituals of mourning.

But thanks to Mum, we would pay Dunedin a visit after all.

We flew into Christchurch and visited the cathedral where Peter's father, Harry, had sung in the choir as a boy. Harry had gained a scholarship to the school because of his singing and had loved it. He was sorry when his father moved them to the very remote Gisborne on the North Island. I lit a candle for Mum within the cool stone walls. We drove to Queenstown, past stunning, postcard compositions of snowy mountains reflected in clear lakes. Crystal-clear air, sharp green and grey hills, pale, wintry blue skies …

Then on to Dunedin. I liked the city but didn't feel a burning desire to pack up and live there. In fact, I'd say that one way to really ruin a holiday is to be looking at a place in terms of moving there. It brings out the judge in you when it need not be there. Peter strutted about as if he owned the place and declared how much he liked it. I was annoyed and wasn't sure how much I did like it and how much of a battle was ahead of me in refusing to move.

We toured the suburbs. Was it Janet Frame who described Dunedin as a place where the rich lived on the hills and looked down on the poor by the beach? We liked the idea of being near the beach, but the plots were tiny. Small houses squashed together side by side. Where was the cafe with the view? The beachside promenade? We drove out to the Otago Peninsula round the bay, sweeping in and out along the flat, curling road. We saw albatrosses at the nature reserve, seals on the rocks, crashing waves from the cliffs south of the city. And came back over the hills: a 'straight' road, but careering up and down over the backbone of a range of steep hills. It was tough country.

I liked Dunedin, but it wasn't like I'd fallen in love with it like some people fall in love with Venice, and, after all, you need a lot of momentum to get over the enormous effort involved in moving. The idea of moving to Dunedin seemed to fade once faced with it 'in the flesh'. Not long afterwards we started looking south of Sydney.

Back in Sydney, on a quiet day by myself, I listened to the recording of Mum's funeral. It was nice to hear it. I wondered how I would sound when I spoke, and was glad to hear a clear and confident voice, if one a little wearied by sadness. The funeral director had suggested recording the service, and he'd put the recorder near where I was sitting, so when it came to the hymns, I had to laugh, as my voice rang loud and clear above the muted singing of the congregation. I sighed a little sigh of relief hearing it was okay, I wasn't slipping in and out of pitch!

I listened to Mum's *Classics 2000* CD again, too, as it was one of just a few of her CDs I'd decided to keep. I hadn't ever listened to the Sarah Brightman track, 'Time to Say Goodbye', all the way to the end. I'd heard part of it that Christmas Eve with Mum, and a few bars down the phone when I asked Sheila to play it, then in the church, as Mum's coffin was brought in. But I was relieved to find the funeral directors obviously had played it all the way through, and I was thankful for their professionalism. Although most of the track was suitably gentle, it ended in an operatic-style crescendo that would have sounded dreadful.

Fiona and I agreed we'd have a carving of a daisy on the top of Mum's tombstone. She'd liked the name; she'd named her dog Daisy. And she liked the flowers too. For all her airs and graces, she liked informal flowers best: daisies, herbs, cottage garden flowers. Fiona was dealing with the stonemasons, but I would find an image of a daisy. I thought it would be easy, but in fact it occupied many days. I hunted through my small collection of gardening books. Nothing. Then I spent a couple of Saturday mornings in the New South Wales State Library. We didn't want a perfectly symmetrical daisy or a cluster of little ones. Eventually I found an image I could photocopy. It was a photograph in a horticultural book. The petals were clear and flopping to one side a little. It was perfect.

Dad and Anne visited us in Sydney the following year. We showed them Thirroul, in the Illawarra, south of Sydney and north of Wollongong, We hadn't made up our minds yet, but there was a possibility we might move there and I wanted them to have a picture in their minds of where we'd be if we did decide to go ahead. In fact, it was a clincher; showing them fixed in our minds what a great place it was and we soon started making plans.

When Mum was alive, when something happened that I knew would make her laugh, I would include it in my next postcard. I wrote at least weekly, often more frequently. At first, after she died, when something happened that I would have told her about, it would make me sad that I could no longer do so. My powers to cheer her up and tell her I was thinking of her were reduced to nothing. After she died, I was surprised that I'd thought of her so often and for a little while, the happy things brought tears because they were yet another reminder that she was gone. But after a while I began to see something else. She liked little dramas, funny things the children said, the extraordinary in the ordinary. I still found myself thinking, oh, Mum would have liked that ... I would have told Mum about that. But it made me think back on her in a slightly different light. It reinforced her sense of humour and her way of taking pleasure in the details of life ... literally up to her last hours. Thinking that she would have liked something now helped me value the little things in my life still.

I had taken a few photos of the flowers on Mum's grave, with the misty fields behind. Brown and green, rolling into the distance. For some reason, for a while, they'd ended up wrapped in one of her silk scarves, in a drawer in my bedroom. I got them out one evening and was looking at them when Felix came over. He was intrigued by the white flower arrangement on the grass. 'Grandma is under the flowers,' he decided. It seemed such a lovely image, I didn't correct him.

One year on, Mum's house had not sold, but had tenants in it, we'd crossed Dunedin off our moving list and had made several visits to Thirroul and Austinmer, to a couple of friends. We liked the small town, with its supermarket, bakers, plant shop, newsagents. The scale was small enough to be able to walk from place to place, you could find a good coffee and it was on the train line to Sydney. With its bushy escarpment and string of beaches, with rocky headlands, it had some magic about it.

I still thought of Mum almost every day. Sometimes I came across a letter she wrote and was amazed at how distinctive handwriting is. I used her reference books regularly. A little 1960s potholder with a tomato image had become one of the most useful items in the house. Peter missed it when it needed washing. He also liked the peg bag I'd retrieved from her cellar—I knew he would! A simple, attractive convenience. Mum's chair—or Grandma's chair—had become the best in the house. Sinking into it, with its shielding wings, was like taking a mini-retreat from the world, whether with a cup of tea or a newspaper, or a child who needed soothing. The 'gone-ness' was still confounding at times. That she wasn't in her little house, doing her tapestry, telling me about a villager's new grandchild, scheming an alteration in the kitchen or the bathroom. That all her worldly goods were scattered.

I had her French carriage clock repaired. It had been her father's and there was a story attached to it. My mother's uncle Bennie had been given it as a gift from one of the men involved in the Tutankhamen discovery in Egypt, Lord Caernarvon. Bennie trained his horses. He'd passed it on to Mary, who'd given it to Seamus. Then, with Mum's connection with Egypt, she inherited it when he died. I couldn't open its brass door at the back, nor could I find a key. I took it to a man who repaired clocks in his home workshop, feeling a little uneasy about leaving it there. He said he'd call me in a few months as he had quite a backlog. As I was leaving, he said it was a nice quality clock, dating from 1920. What a shame the chiming mechanism had been taken out, he said. ('That'd be right,' Máire commented later. Their dad hated chimes and would have had no compunction in removing it.) The man would repair it and craft a new key. I picked it up six months later but was a little worried when I got it home, wound it up and it would not start. It had cost several hundred dollars to repair. Was I going to have to take it back? Then Peter reminded me of the clockmaker's figure-of-eight twist. I tried, holding the clock firmly and sure enough, the fast ticking began, and through the glass on the top, under the handle, you could now see the mechanism swiftly moving left and right, like a beating heart.

Dad sent a picture of Mum's grave on the anniversary of her death. It wouldn't have been up all that long. You have to wait for the ground to settle. It's a lovely tombstone. She'd have liked it, I think. It has the Oscar Wilde lines she wanted, and the daisy. I couldn't help thinking of her from time to time six foot under in her little room. It was a thought I'd rather not have had. Then the images returned that were with me in the dawns after the news—a thin, birdish lady, wearing thick jumpers, stirring a saucepan in her kitchen, tasting a concoction with a dip of the finger. The backdrop was of her last few years, in the house she lived in alone. But the face was earlier, before she was sick. Before it became puffy. Then I saw her at the back of the houses, arms folded against the cool air, a brave smile 'goodbye' as we waved. I remembered the paperiness of her skin, feeling a slight irritation with her tiredness, piling things into the car—boys, toys, what else?—as I always seemed to be doing. You never know when the last time you see someone will turn out to be. Looking back, you see it and it's amazing to observe in retrospect how you were trundling along, oblivious, not knowing what was coming your way.

Friends invited us to stay in their house in Thirroul for a few days over Christmas while they were overseas. It was a good opportunity to get to know the area more. If Mum had been alive, I would have written something like this:

> Dear Mum
>
> We've seen a house that we like in Thirroul. We're staying at Susan and Johnny's over Christmas for a couple of nights and saw it from the outside. It looks big enough and is just 12 minutes walk from the town centre. It's a bit run-down looking and has two palm trees by the front steps. We were having a drink at the pub and we wondered about the garden, so I walked quickly back to have a peep. We didn't think it was inhabited. I peeped round the drive at the back and came face to face with a goat! A white tethered goat. Whose goat was it? The real estate office is closed over Christmas, so I guess we won't find out for a while.
>
> Love from Alison

We missed out on that house. To be honest, it was shocking inside. It had a lovely garden, with a stone wall and a small tree that provided dappled shade. But inside the walls were dreadful, the bathroom cracked, the lino on the kitchen floor worn through. By then we'd seen a few houses, however, and there wasn't much around. It did have character, it wasn't halfway up a hill to the escarpment, it was a short walk to the station and the rent was a fraction of what we'd get for our house in Sydney. By the time Peter had persuaded me that we should take it, another couple had nabbed it.

We were so disappointed. Friends pointed out that we hadn't been one hundred per cent sure about it and perhaps it was for the best. But the new school year was fast approaching. Harry had left the school in Surry Hills and one way or another was going to start school in Thirroul. We had to find somewhere to live.

I was determined not to miss another house. I'd already made a list of the twenty or so real estate agents that dealt with lettings in the area. I decided I would call them every morning. We wanted a three-bedroom house with a garden in Thirroul, or, I began to think, the next suburb, Austinmer. Some of the agents began to recognise my voice. It didn't matter. I wanted to be the first to know if something came up. A cottage with a small garden but not a garage was going to be vacant at the end of January in Austinmer. We wanted to see it as soon as possible. We arranged through the agent to view it, even though the tenant was still there. We rocked up to Central Station only to find that trains were off, buses on. No one could tell us what time the buses arrived. We tried to get hold of the agent. No reply. We didn't know the tenant's name or number.

We decided to rent a car. Peter got on the phone, and about half an hour later we were setting off from a rental place in Kings Cross. By the time we arrived in Austinmer we were an hour late. The house was in a quiet, no-through road. It looked about eighty years old, weatherboard with a big wraparound verandah. We couldn't believe it. It was just what we'd been looking for. We hoped the tenant was still in. She was. 'I was expecting you an hour ago,' she said, not too impressed. But she softened once we explained about the trains. In fact, the house was only a few metres from the train line. 'What are the trains like?' we asked. (You couldn't tell that day because they weren't on!) Noisy, but you get used to them, was the answer. We loved the inside too, with its wood panelling and polished floorboards.

We swung into action and soon secured it. Moved in the day before school started. Moving was a nightmare as usual and took two vanloads as the removalists had not brought the big one as promised on the first day. But the fact they went down to the beach for a swim after they'd moved our stuff in confirmed the fact we'd chosen a lovely place to live.

Mum would have loved the incidental coincidences about our move: the fact that the tenant was from Christchurch, and that when she had moved from New Zealand, she'd found the cottage on the internet and only after making the arrangements did she find out that her cousins lived two doors up; that Susan and Johnny ended up buying a house in Woonona, two suburbs south of Thirroul from a couple that bought the house next to us in Redfern. That a lady on our tiny street recognised me as a customer of a shop she'd helped get going in Surry Hills.

Mum was in my dreams. I had another vivid dream about her in the months following our move. She was bed-ridden and terminally ill and, I think, beyond communication. I was due to travel. There was lots to do with planes, luggage and timetables. We knew Mum was going to die and there was an expectation that we gave her something just before I went, like euthanasia, I thought. The knowledge of this was very worrying and a heavy burden. Then at the very last minute we decided not to give it to her and I went away feeling lighter, with a little relief, as it meant there was a sliver of a chance I might see her again when I came back.

Sometimes when I turned the tap on first thing in the morning to fill the kettle I thought of a conversation with Mum at Hawkhurst. The water must have been turned off for some time. When someone came to reconnect it or fix it, he told her that when you hadn't used water in a house for a long time you should let it run out of the tap for a while to flush out water that's been sitting in the pipes. I remember her sharing that piece of information with me like a bit of juicy gossip.

A couple of months after moving in, the sun is streaming through the kitchen windows, through Mum's crystal, picking out the spiders' webs on the sills outside. Rainbows dance on the walls, the fridge, a deep one has slipped into the dark, small sitting room. Cobalt, coral, lemon glow on gloss paint over the fireplace. Harry and Felix stand bewitched, looking up at the dancing light. Oscar, black coat gleaming, plays with a ball of light on the floor, trying to catch it with white-tipped paws, back arching, tail swishing. For a moment we are fixed on that lovely light shining through and transformed by the crystal glinting at the window.

The crystal bewitches us in our own home as it once shone in Mum's. Oscar's grown. He's no toe-biting kitten anymore, but a sleek, elegant young cat.

Oscar loved the new house, once he was let out. The hunting was good, though not so good for us. We found a little mouse on the path outside in the early weeks. Peter buried it and Harry made a grave marker with thin cardboard that was gold on one side. 'Here lies a mouse thought to have died from cat attack,' he wrote. Felix was quite taken with the event too and asked me to write on a similar piece of cardboard: 'The mouse was killed by a cat named Oscar,' with a separate marker saying, 'The mouse is under the dirt.'

The immediacy of Mum's death gradually faded, but writing about it brought back some of the intensity. Writing about the lowering of my mother's coffin into the hole, tears choke me up as they've not done for a long while. But it's the living who pervade my life. Ever looking at my watch, I break in time to pick up my boys from school.

Writing this is a new experience. I'm still dealing with facts. But personal facts, veiled by memory, coloured with feelings. I break from writing about my parents' split to be at the last twenty minutes of Harry's soccer match. I ignore the squabblings over a Tazo, or some other trivial toy, as I write about seeing my mother's body.

Sometimes when I found my maternal role a challenge, I wondered about my own mother. With some of my own domestic rage brewing—endless cleaning, mindless picking-up after people, the thankless task of holding the household together—I wondered whether she felt smothered by being a wife and a mother. Did she feel frustration? Is that why she drank?

One evening I was leafing through one of Mum's poetry books. I was really happy to be able to add a few of Mum's poetry books to my own collection. Apparently, poetry readers—especially people who go so far as to buy collections of poetry—are a relatively rare species. Although in some cultures, the poem is more valued than in others. I'm thinking of Haiku, which evolved from a sort of game where people recited short verses. My collection includes a volume of Australian poetry, some French verses, a three-volume boxed set of English poetry, and many children's rhymes and poems. A new volume of the Persian poet, Rimu. Why do people think poetry is stuffy? It's so often a play with language and words, rhythms that make you smile, images that clear away the mundane. I like it for its brain effect—and that you can dip into it, open up a book, read a few lines and have welcomed in an original thought, a new way of looking at the world.

I was looking for poems about the sea, perhaps to incorporate into some artists' books I was planning on making. I came across one called 'Ode', by A. W. E. O'Shaughnessy. Number 396 in the little red poetry book, which on closer inspection turns out to be an edition of *Palgrave's Golden Treasury*. The volume was first published in 1861, under the title *The Golden Treasury of the Best Songs and Lyrical Poems in the English Language, Selected and arranged by Francis Turner Palgrave*. It appears to have been quite a publishing success story. New editions with additional poems were published from 1907 onwards. Mum's appeared to be a 1957 edition, the last poem is 'This Bread I Break' by Dylan Thomas. *Palgrave's Treasury* is still in print today, with a sixth edition published in 2002 and new entries that pad its pages to around 700. Its most recent publishers describe it as one of the best-loved and most frequently bought poetry anthologies of all time.

So here is Shakespeare: 'Crabbed age and youth cannot live together:' ... 'Age, I do abhor thee;/ Youth, I do adore thee;', Gray's 'On A Favourite Cat, Drowned In A Tub of Goldfishes', Wordsworth and Shelley on skylarks (do people still write poems about skylarks? I find myself wondering). Mum's pencil notes are scattered sparsely throughout the book. This was the book that alerted us to Mum's Eleanore (with an 'e') phase, and faded ink at the frontispiece says 'Eleanore McGonigle, Form V'. Her writing just the same as the last letter she wrote, but did not finish, to me. Many of the annotations explain words like 'hymeneal': next to it, Mum wrote, 'Hymen, God of marriage.' Strange to think of a young girl learning about such a god. Did he (or she?) look out for her?

But the verse which first captured my attention, in O'Shaughnessy's 'Ode' was:

We are the music-makers,
And we are the dreamers of dreams,
Wandering by lone sea-breakers,
And sitting by desolate streams;
World-losers and world-forsakers,
On whom the pale moon gleams:
Yet we are the movers and shakers
Of the world for ever, it seems.

The rest of the poem is not as catchy. I'd never heard of him so looked him up on the internet. He's a Victorian poet, born in 1844 in London, who worked in the fields of reptiles and fish at the British Museum and the Natural History Museum. His friends included members of the

Pre-Raphaelite Brotherhood and he married a woman called Eleanor (without an 'e'). He died of a chill in 1881, which would have made him thirty-seven, give or take a birthday. *The Cambridge Guide to Literature in English* notes that he is usually only remembered for his 'delicate "Ode" in Music and Moonlight beginning "We are the music-makers".'

Mr O'Shaughnessy may be largely forgotten, but his poetry lives on, it seems. Someone I come across on the internet says the first two lines appear in the film *Willy Wonka and the Chocolate Factory*—I'll have to watch it now to verify his claim! And the phrase 'movers and shakers', which seems so modern—and not at all about the poets that O'Shaughnessy refers to—is attributed to his poem. Added to that, the 'Ode' was set to music by Elgar.

Flicking through some other poetry books one evening, I picked up Mum's copy of a Pocket Poet edition of Hopkins. Gerard Manley Hopkins. I'm beginning to forget, I note, which books were Mum's and which not. When I chose things from her house, I wanted them to blend after a while and become as much ours as hers. I liked the idea of a wooden spoon from her kitchen being used in ours, becoming something we reached for without thinking too much about its origin. So I guess I wanted this to happen with her books too. I have such an eclectic collection: I pick them up from markets, bookstores, other people ... I'm quite glad she put her name in a lot of them, although this might have been more of a habit earlier on in her life. This one has her name (without the extra 'e' by now) inside. I must admit I was slightly horrified at her nerve in putting her name inside a leatherbound edition of Tennyson, under the original owner. But in another way, what's wrong with that?

There are some slips of paper inside the Hopkins, where, incidentally, I note there is a poem about a skylark—a caged one. One postcard-sized note is a receipt for 10 lessons in speech and drama, £6.60, dated 26.9.67 from a lady in Sevenoaks; another is a 'score' card from an examination for the London Academy of Music and Dramatic Art. It's the Acting Bronze Medal, which she took on 19 Jul 1967 (stamped in red ink), at 3.15. She was number 500. She got 8 out of 10 for make-up and grooming, 18 out of 25 for naturalness and spontaneity, 16 out of 20 for movement; a third piece of paper is a typed carbon copy notice for the Seal Poetry Group which she used to help run. It's dated Autumn 1967. On Sept. 28th they were doing Walt Whitman and Coventry Patmore. They met fortnightly, it seemed. Gerard Manley Hopkins was down for Nov. 23rd.

I feel quite moved holding these little pieces of evidence about Mum's earlier life. My sister and I would only have been two and four respectively. I now know what an effort it is to look after young children and how you can lose contact with the things you love. So I admire my 1967 mother for taking a drama exam, running a poetry society and having drama lessons as well as making green jelly for our birthday parties (as a bed for pear hedgehogs with cloves for spikes).

Sometimes on a Saturday, in those months after moving to Austinmer, I managed to squeeze a drop of time alone into my week. After a cup of tea over a book (what bliss) I took off on my bike. Alone. Sometimes I headed north, up and down the winding coast road. Sometimes I headed south, past the houses and lawns to the bike path and the flat, wave-beaten sandy beaches. Alternatively I would cycle then get off and walk. Sometimes I'd see a swimmer in the rock swimming pools, with a handsome dog guarding a pile of weekend wear. Other times I read the names of the gravestones in Wombarra, working out the age at death, gleaning what personal story I could from a few words and dates. The first time I visited the Wombarra Cemetery, on a beautiful grassy headland with waves crashing on a rock platform below, the graves at the front of the cemetery, looking out to sea, seemed to be the most recent. The dead are slowly marching towards the water, I thought grimly. I was relieved when I walked back up to where I'd locked my bike, near the road, that in fact the ages of graves were mixed. A much healthier state of affairs.

One afternoon I caught the 4.56 train up to Sydney for a 'girls' night out' at a Thai restaurant. By the end of the evening, just three of us remained at the table. The three of us, it turned out, had mothers who were alcoholics. 'I just remember opening cupboards, opening doors and there would be a glass of wine. Opening cupboards … glass of sherry or something in the laundry … in the kitchen,' said one whose line was, 'I wonder if there was something else with my mother, not just the alcoholism … ' The other said she believed in an alcoholic gene and having had one glass of wine too many herself, got teary talking about why she hadn't had children—that she was worried about carrying on the gene. But while I see my mother's drinking as a symptom of something wrong, I don't see it as something that was bound to happen. And it's not how I define her. Her alcoholism, drinking problem, whatever you want to call it, is not all there is to know about her … it wrecked her marriage, ruined her health, left her partially disabled and robbed her prematurely of her life … but it wasn't the only thing about her and I feel I owe it to her to remember the good things and the whole person, not just her drinking. I don't like the label, either. There are a thousand and one reasons why people drink too much and become addicted to it, and as many patterns in their lives. It's a complex matter with no pat answer.

But of course, I do find myself wondering about what went on in my mother's head, and about mothers in general and the differences and similarities between our experiences as mothers. Did she sometimes drown in domestic high water? How often did she feel compelled to wash the kitchen floor? Was she like me, determined somewhere in the back of her mind to believe that floors only need cleaning once a week? Even when confronted with evidence to the contrary. Or did it start out as a game for grown-ups—a young adult, thrown into the life of a housewife and so soon afterwards a mother? Actually, appearances were genuinely important to her, so I think housework came fairly easily. But for a while there, she lost sight of the rest—the intimacy, reaching out to others—that really matters to our hearts.

I remember as a child seeing a photograph of her when I was a baby. She was looking at me the way people look at newborns—full of love and laughter. I remember being surprised inside at her looking so happy. She wasn't an affectionate mother but she loved us in the ways she could. We had beige tights for Brownies, tried ballet and tap, we were driven around second-hand riding shops for new hats, jodhpurs and hacking jackets. There was a good tea ready for us when we got back from school. A light meal like toast toppers—a dog's dinner look-alike that you spread on toast and grilled. Do they still exist? Little cakes or chocolate biscuits—Penguins, Club biscuits, mini chocolate-covered swiss rolls. Later she could always be relied upon to put on a good spread for a family gathering. 'She wasn't a very loving mother,' my father once said to me as an adult. That may have been, but by the time she died, I did feel loved by her. I didn't doubt it although I didn't consider her the perfect role model in any way. But I don't believe in perfection. And I think a lot of that mother–daughter stuff is the stuff of myths. It's a hard role.

But parts of it she no doubt wanted to embrace, or thought she did. I did think she'd have been happier with a career; a drama teacher, or interior designer, maybe something to do with history. Sometimes she seemed selfish, self-centred, but she never did anything really big for herself. I admired her for her attention to detail and for the pleasure she took in little things but I know I need to transcend these as well. I want to shut out domestic, family life chatter at times and feel part of something bigger.

I think of my dinner companion's description of opening cupboards and finding sherry ... I think of my mother's house at the end of her life. Opening cupboards and hoping to uncover a secret, a clue, something that sheds light on why it all happened. Why her life took the course it did.

Looking through her house. Opening drawers, emptying baskets ... tapestry in here, soap and bath salts there ... a box of alternative medicines, old clothes, tea towels, glass jars ... a rusted icing set in its original box. Hoping to find a clue to how she was feeling, what she was really thinking ... The cellar smelt damp. We looked in cardboard boxes ... we'd be getting house clearers in so we didn't want to miss something that one of us should have kept. Hoping to unravel the secrets of our mother's life. We found a Roman Catholic missal, covered in white-and-green mould, buried deep in an old bathroom basket with a cushioned top. I wiped it clean. The pages were fine and heavy and it was filled with little prayer cards with dedications written in joined but youthful handwriting, 'Dear Eleanore ... ' The extra 'e' again.

I struggled a little with the fact that alcohol had done so much damage to my mother's body. She had drunk too much for her own good, obviously, but in terms of volumes,

I suspected it was not that much compared to many other heavy drinkers. When I got back to Sydney after Mum's funeral, I saw the familiar street people whose lives were soaked in cheap sherry or even meths. They slept in doorways and bus shelters. Had purple skin and torn clothes. How were these people still alive, but my mother dead? There was one in particular I called Death. He was so pale, his skin almost disappearing like a ghost's. He wore a checked, dark-green suit jacket that looked as if it would not come off. When I visited my doctor in Surry Hills, I told her what I'd been thinking. Having many of these people as patients, she said she couldn't help agreeing. Sometimes a patient would come back year after year, and by all logic, their bodies should not be able to keep going, but they do.

Not eating was half of it, I knew that. And the other? The fact that different bodies react in different ways. What one can handle year in, year out, sets another on biochemical warfare.

In the winter at Austinmer I was often up while it was still dark. If I was up early enough, looking out the back steps there'd be a big white star midway in the sky to the north. My usual routine was to turn the heater on, lift up the blind in the sitting room, fill the kettle and boot up my computer. One morning, I don't think I saw the star that time, the kettle was heating the water for my two cups of tea. Peter was still in bed, I'd take him a cup of tea soon. I'd started my computer, had logged on and was downloading new email messages. Mum's poetry book was on my desk as I'd been writing about it and looking up some of the poets on the internet. I was holding it and turning pages. I'd come to a few pages with Mum's pencilled notes on them. The messages were downloading and my computer made a rumbling noise which sounded exactly like my mother's voice, it seemed to say in a flat tone she sometimes had, 'Hello, Alison.' That's all. The 'receiving messages' circled arrow continued to spin, and a few moments later a few more messages sat in the in-box. My heart jumped and I felt a prickly feeling all round my chest. Writing about it now, I can hardly believe it happened—and by that I don't mean that I heard my mother's voice, but even that I heard a sound which sounded like my mother's voice. I didn't take too much notice afterwards, and carried on with the morning's tasks. But later I told Peter I'd had a strange experience. I wasn't sure if he'd think I was mad, but he took me seriously. 'I don't really think it was her voice,' I said. 'But it was very strange.' I felt hot and a few tears welled in my eyes as I told him.

He left to go to Borneo on a work-related trip later that day and referred to it in an email he sent. I answered:

Yes, it was strange about my computer's voice sounds. On the one hand you can say I was in a mindset to interpret a gurgle-type noise as a voice, particularly my mother's. As I said, I was holding the little red poetry book which had some of her handwriting on it. On the other, I can't help thinking that some people would say it was her—and with an imagination and a mind that is at least willing to allow itself to think things without necessarily believing them one way or another, it does open up the possibility of at least imagining a scenario where there is another dimension—but if there is, it is hard for communication to occur between the two planes. Most of me doesn't believe this, but another part says, how do I know, really? and yet another, at the same time, is aware of the myriad of stories old and new which explore this possibility. So whether you believe it or not, it seems to be such a human thing to at least entertain the possibility that the dead can somehow reach us.

As I write this, the book I'm reading is *Seven Types of Ambiguity* by Elliot Perlman. The last few pages I was reading were about poetry, and language separating us from animals ... and ambiguity. Well, here's another shade of it. A life—who's to say what it was all about. Is the way you look at your own life how others regard it too? Or do they interpret it another way? To Sheila, my mother was a sister who listened without judgement, who had stories and gossip to tell, thoughtful gifts to give ... to a friend's mother, Mum's life appeared tragic ... to others she appeared coldly independent, not needing people in depth ... to some she was cruel, to some thoughtful and kind. To Fiona and me, her daughters, a sharp, sometimes bitter, mixture of all these.

Many of Mum's books that I'd claimed had an almost mythical aura to them. I'd seen their covers since I was old enough to notice them and read their spines: *The Blue-Fly in His Head*; *A Prospect of the Sea*, with its milky-blue wave pattern. But I have no memory of seeing her read them, nor was it anything we ever talked about. I don't even remember really looking inside these books. But I regarded them as special and still do. Oddly, it was only two years after Mum's death that I really looked through them. Peter picked up the copy of *The Blue-Fly in his Head* and opened it by chance on a poem with the title 'Household Devils': 'Possessed by the little household devils/That grimace at me from recalcitrant objects'—it fitted nicely with Peter's theory of the innate hostility of inanimate objects. The nasty little things that disappear when you most need them.

I looked up the poem in the Hopkins, 'Caged Skylark': '... Man's mounting spirit in his bone-house, mean house, dwells—'. It talks of drudgery, day-labouring out life's age. Tied to the kitchen sink? Slaving over a hot stove? Brooms and picking up, picking up, mostly after other people. That's my version of drudgery.

I had another look at some of the other books I'd taken from her collection. There was a *Rhymes and Jingles, For Practice in Speech Training*. I thought Harry might enjoy some of the tongue-twisters like this one:

Sue sifteth cinders through a shovel-shaped sifter,
Through a shovel-shaped sifter those cinders she sifteth.
Those cinders Sue sifteth, she sifteth, she sifteth,
Those cinders Sue sifteth till the sifting she finisheth.

A real tongue-twister. See how quickly you can say it without getting the sounds mixed up.

In this electronic age, do children even know what cinders are? We had open fires as children—I remember being really upset once because I threw my hanky on the fire thinking it was a tissue instead. But we had fan heaters and radiators too; we just liked the comfort of a flame, I think.

And another one:

Shopping
I go to the greengrocer:
'Beetroot please,
Rhubarb please,
Thank you.'

This is an exercise for the lips and jaw. The mouth must be well open for 'I'; wide and then rounded for 'greengrocer' and 'beetroot'; rounded and then well open for 'rhubarb'.

Other gems are to be found in *Manners and Movements In Costume Plays*. It is marked on the pale-green and brown-tinged cover, in pencil, '6/-'. Six shillings. Among them, advice about using a snuff-box à la nineteenth century: 'Take the snuff-box in the left hand (note the turn of the wrist); tap the lid with the right forefinger ... '

And—should you be wearing a farthingale, hoop or crinoline—be sure to keep the waist in the centre of the circle when moving. 'A sway from side to side is definitely ugly.'

I realise these books belong to Mum's myth—her family story that we swallowed without much questioning. Wouldn't it be nice to be able to ask her more now: about how she was going to be a drama teacher, and about meeting my father—in Switzerland of all places, both on skiing holidays (the first and last? I don't ever remember hearing of either of them skiing again). The story of how Grandpa Mac refused to sign the form unless she stopped seeing my father. I don't think he had anything particular against Dad—it may have been that he didn't want Mum to leave school, or to get married too young.

At the end of her schooling she had a collection of O Levels and various certificates in drama and piano. She told me how she refused to be swayed by her father and went to live in Hastings. It was her act of defiance, daredevil, show of independence. When I first heard it I probably didn't make much of it. As the facts seeped in later, I used to think it was a shame she'd taken it that way—that she would have been so much happier had she had a career of sorts. Couldn't she have pretended not to see Dad for a while? She considered she'd done some impressive fighting then. I wasn't as impressed as she'd have liked, had she known what

I thought. I wished she'd fought for something or other for a bit longer.

Of course, I now realise how hard it is to hang on to something resembling a career. I can't claim to have got it all perfect myself. And all the moving around they did would hardly have helped. But these books of Mum's, that I remember being around as a child, yet weren't opened in my presence, are to me reminders that she did try.

Dear Mum

Peter was in Borneo this weekend. I had a 'catch up' day in the house. Didn't do as much as I'd hoped— only really got the washing-up done—but took the boys out to Coledale market too. I've been knitting Felix a scarf out of that very fluffy wool and Harry and Felix said they'd like to learn. I went to a shop a few weeks ago but they didn't have any fat wool. But at the market I bought some chunky needles and some lovely red wool with blue blobs. So we've been knitting: Felix sits on my lap and does a few stitches. Harry seemed to be OK on his own after a little lesson. But in four rows he's gained 10 stitches! I don't know how so I'm going to have to do some knitting spying, I told him!

Dear Mum

Felix said something yesterday about a telescope and I thought he meant microscope, so I got out the one that Granddad gave me years ago. The sponge that must have sat over all the slides had disintegrated crumbly so it was a bit of a mess but we wiped a few slides and got out a lamp. We've been looking at peanut butter, Vegemite, honey, saliva. We've seen sharp thorn-like things on the side of grass. 'Wow!' says Felix. He's always liked tiny things. Today I found a tick on Oscar's ear. Peter had already taken the boys to school. I put it under the microscope and I looked at it at 100 times magnification. It was moving and you could see sucker-like attachments on the end of its endlessly wriggling legs. They opened and closed like tiny parachutes. Peter had a look too. Half an hour later I went to look at it and it had gone! It had managed to crawl out from under the tiny glass cover. I thought it couldn't have gone far and sure enough it was on the underside of the slide holder. Now it's back on its slide, covered, with a piece of Sellotape over the top. I'm hoping it's still alive when Felix and Harry come home.

I thought back over Mum's life and our family life. When I was pregnant with Harry I was interviewed as part of a woman's research into postnatal depression. The interviewer asked about the family I was from and the sort of family I wanted to create. I wanted—and still do want—a more open family life than I experienced. I want my children to have the means to talk to me about important things, personal things, how they feel about their lives and how I feel about mine. And by 'means' I suppose I'm talking partly about the habit—a well-worn path that they can tread. It was virtually impossible to talk to Mum about the really big things—her marriage for one, and her drinking for two. I thought back to when I'd mentioned to Dad that I was concerned about her drinking. He'd said something to her— he was in Texas at the time and she was back in England for a break. She didn't speak to me for months. Why didn't I say something directly to her? I had tried. We had all tried. Directly or indirectly, coming to a subject obliquely, approaching it gently, coming in the side gate, so to speak. But the reaction was almost always the same—the gate was locked. There was no path.

And we sometimes felt, looking back, that when we were young children she wasn't very good at showing her love for us. But I knew, at least as an adult, I had no doubt, that she did love my sister and me. And I never felt that I was short-changed on the love front: there was plenty around, from Dad, from aunts, grandparents especially.

But I guess I'd like my boys to be absolutely sure about the fact I love them. I make sure I tell them—the words get rusty and awkward if you don't use them often.

One night when he was still a preschooler, Felix said to me, with a big grin, as if he was clever to have made the realisation, 'When I'm grown up, you will die.' He said it again, 'When Harry and I are grown up, you will die, and Daddy will die.' He was quite taken with the idea, but the more he thought about it, the sadder he became—the grin gave way to, 'And it's making me sad.'

I'd been thinking about Mum, so was feeling a little sad myself. 'Yes, I will die, but you might be very grown-up, we'll do things together when you're a grown-up and I'm a grown-up,' I tried to console him. 'You can take me out to lunch for my birthday.' Eventually he fell asleep on my lap, his arms around my neck, his head on my shoulder.

We had another family holiday in New Zealand.

Dear Mum
We're in Paraparaumu with Peter's mum. Harry is playing with a new toy, an Astrojax—like a very

sophisticated yoyo with three balls. Felix is thrilled with a little torch that can flash red and when you slide a piece of plastic across, turns white. I thought of you yesterday at the Te Papa museum—a lovely light-filled, busy museum in Wellington. In one of the displays in the room about volcanoes, tectonic plates, earthquakes and the like there was a clock face with man at twelve o'clock, dinosaurs, start of life etc. Daisies came into being between 25 and 30 million years ago, it said. It reminded me of you and your love of daisies.

Dear Mum

We had a daft sort of evening yesterday. Peter had been in Sydney for various things including a dentist's appointment and was catching a train that stopped at Thirroul. (He could have got the one that stopped at Austinmer ten minutes later.) He had his computer with him so asked if I could pick him up. At 7.45 Harry, Felix and I jumped in the car to meet him. The steering felt a bit odd in Thirroul and when I turned the car to park it at the station I realised we had a flat tyre. The train was late and Harry had a riddle for Peter: 'We drove to meet you but we can't drive back. Why?' We made slow progress into the town and decided to stop for pizzas. Afterwards Harry rolled the trundler suitcase home, I carried leftover pizza and Peter gave Felix a piggyback and we finally got home at quarter to ten!

Around two years after Mum died, I couldn't help thinking of all the little things in our lives that she didn't know about. She didn't know we moved. She didn't get to hear about any of the three books of mine that had been published since she died. She didn't know I dedicated one to her. She hadn't heard about Felix's little revolution one fortnight when he started swimming lessons and violin and Nippers. She didn't hear about our New Zealand holidays or the fun and games removing ticks from Oscar now that he's semi 'bush'!

Two years on, I talked a lot about her and thought about her a lot. But it was usually without tears. I wasn't pulling her back with my grief. I was letting her float out in her coracle. I read her books. I still felt a big swell of love for my mother. I still went over in my head what her life was like and tried to remember details to write down. At one point I remember thinking. What do I know about my mother? That she liked liquorice allsorts (something I learnt only as an adult and which totally surprised me!) and cold toast. The latter was part of our childhood mythology about her. At boarding school cold toast was what you got at breakfast and she'd become used to it to such a degree it became what she preferred. Sometimes I felt I knew so little about her. I thought about the picture of her on her bicycle as a five- or six-year-old, maybe seven. She has a cocky look on her face. Her shoes look big. It's a black-and-white shot, the location looks maybe a bit rough behind. She wasn't keen on Ireland like her sisters. Was it the 'poor girl from Ireland among all the rich kids at the convent' syndrome?

When we were growing up, she was hopeless talking about anything 'girlie' like periods or bras, or, later, boyfriends. In fact, she just totally avoided the subjects. When I was around twelve, a cushion-like package of sanitary towels appeared mysteriously in my wardrobe. The white wooden wardrobe with smooth long handles that Mum had in her cellar at Burwash. I assumed the pads were Mum's. They were the old-fashioned fat variety with a thin stretchy belt to hold them up. Mum never mentioned them or periods, birds and bees or anything remotely to do with reproduction. There'd been a book with illustrations like paper cutouts of female and male bodies, sperms, eggs, babies being born. Then later a booklet about spots and periods, with pictures of girls playing tennis and generally looking healthy. I gleaned information—like lots of girls, I guess—from babysitters, sixteen-year-olds at the recreation ground or the bus stop and other older girls 'in the know'. (And, more explicitly from a copy of Desmond Morris's *The Naked Ape*, which left nothing to the imagination.)

It's so ridiculous what you do remember. I remember a conversation between my mother and Brown Owl (I enjoyed Brownies but not Guides, where I only lasted two weeks because we cleaned brass both weeks and were going to clean the toilets the next ... I thought there were better ways to spend after-school evenings). They were in the spacious hall at our house in Ightham that had the antique carved chest where I coloured an elaborate flower poster one Christmas, and a big square patterned carpet. A piano had stood for a while by one wall and Mum had tried to teach Fiona and me to play, but not for long—she got fed up, or we did ... I don't know but it seems a shame, I wish she'd persevered. The black phone with its heavy receiver and rotary dial used to sit there. You had to call the operator and ask to be connected. I once called a friend and she was calling me at the same time, so we were put together by the operator. Mum and Brown Owl, a woman with short dark hair and fat knees, were discussing uniforms and the beige tights I wore with my brown dress were praised and my mother said something about making the effort to look smart.

I suppose it reminds me of the busy childhood we had. Busy in a good way, I mean. My parents arranged, paid for and made possible lots of activities. For a few years we had French students come to stay in the house for a few weeks. There was a terribly thin girl—they seemed like women to me—but I guess they were in their teens. She had a mass of shoulder-length frizzy dark hair. She wore narrow-legged jeans and a sheepskin waistcoat with embroidered flowers on it. While she sat at the dinner table with us, she never seemed to eat anything and appeared to survive on black coffee. (She didn't look healthy on it either.) Another I remember being called 'bébé' by an equally mature-seeming male, who was perhaps sixteen. She wrote in my autograph book, 'Alison is always good to those who come home.'

I don't know, but I have the feeling that Brownies, French exchange students and later going to France myself was driven by my mother. It would be normal, I suppose, looking at it another way, just as I'm the one organising swimming lessons, violin tuition, Nippers, friends over, etc. etc. for my children. We did Brownies, we were very involved with the local riding school (which would have come from Dad), we had a go at ballet and tap. (I can still impress with a single movement that involves quite a bit of tipping and tapping. I've no idea why I can still do that but only that, I guess it has a pleasing sound and feeling!)

Mum made me a long skirt, when they were fashionable, with a triangular section at the waist and ties at the back. It was black check with some red flowers over the top. I wore it with a 'skinny rib' to Beatrice Parson's tenth birthday party.

Death is so natural, yet we don't often talk of it openly. For me, talking and writing about my mother's death has made me feel quite easy about talking to others who are dealing with near and dear ones close to death. I can't say that I necessarily face the idea of my own death with greater ease. I feel very needed by my family and I don't want to go just yet. And it's not that I'm hardened to it either. My eyes water as I read of the death of a man I never met, on the other side of the world. My husband's friend went back to Scotland to be with his dad and as a way of keeping in touch, sent friends the jokes and little stories of his past. Peter passed on to me the last email, which told how he'd helped his dad up the stairs one night and he died quickly in his arms.

I hear of death 'stories' and in the way that they are each different and special, I'm reminded of birth stories. Stories full of the little details that matter so much, which tell of how someone came into the world. Perhaps we all have the same need to hear about the bookends, those passages that mark the beginning and end of someone's life.

When a friend's mother died at eighty-six, her youngest sister said, 'We'd had her so long.' Barbara described how they brought her mother's body back to her house after she'd died in hospital. They put her in her bed and people could 'go in for a chat'. I thought that was a comforting idea. Barbara said it made the transition easier, more gentle. I thought in comparison of my visit to my Mum's body, in a strange little room, a few minutes and never to be seen again.

Death comes up more readily in conversations now. I'm not sure if that's good or not. I guess it's good. Felix talked about 'when your Mum was shot' which rather shocked me. So we talked about how she died peacefully in her sleep because her body was sick and she was tired and ready to die. We talked of his granddad, Harry senior, too ('My granddad was a soldier!') and how he died. Felix thinks over these things. One morning out of the blue he said, 'My granddad had a nice death.' Yes. His last few days had been tough, but he'd died basically because of old age and up until those last days had been fit and active.

I'm not alone in thinking that a child's death would be the hardest to face, and when my children have minor illnesses, colds and flus, it's never far away in my mind, how lucky I am to have healthy kids, how heartbreaking it must be to have really sick children, or ones with conditions you know will only deteriorate.

It's all a reminder of the ordinary miracles that pervade everyday life. The fact that I sit here twitching my fingers, watching spidery letters appear on a white page on a computer screen, is amazing enough. But what about the sparks going off in my head, the nerve impulses driving these thoughts and actions, the blood pounding in my ears, my heart, my fingers, the breath of life in and out of my lungs. Outside, I hear a bird in a tree I know will be wet with rain. Without looking, I know the escarpment is a dark brooding green and there'll be white wisps of mist hanging above the trees. Waking briefly one morning at five, I saw the full moon just about to set behind the escarpment while on the ocean side of the house, a peach sky filled with the sunrise.

Dear Mum
We have a possum in the traveller's palm. He runs
over the corrugated roof at night and crashes around
the giant leaves searching for the pale green-and-blue
spiky flowers. I found him in a torch beam and he
looked down at us. Furry and grey with a black fluffy

tail. Last night bright green cicadas crashed onto the verandah with veined glass-like wings. They didn't fly away, so Felix and Kathleen were thrilled to be able to pick them up.

A friend asked if I was writing about the relationship between my mother and myself: the 'mother–daughter relationship'. And people ask, 'were you close?' as if it's a measure of the depth of my sadness about her death. I can try to express and describe the relationship I have with my mother, Eleanor, but to label it 'mother–daughter' and measure it against some benchmark, I find tricky. I can say, we did this, we did that, I could tell her this, I couldn't tell her that. She was quick to tell me I was a good mother. She was impressed that I took my children to galleries, parks ... out and about. And that I didn't 'park' them in front of the TV. Were she and I close? We loved each other. She was aware of my support, probably of some disapproval too ... what does it mean to be close? How do you define it? Is there a measure? How do you weigh up just how much you care for someone? How intimate you are. Perhaps that's an important nub: the word intimacy. Were you intimate? Not particularly. 'Close' is a less demanding quality; whereas 'intimate' suggests sharing of feelings and confidences.

The trouble with 'mother–daughter' is that once you use those words, rather than Eleanor and Alison, you bring expectations. What 'should' that relationship bring: nurturing of body and mind, sharing of love, positive role modelling? These weighty expectations are difficult to live up to.

I found a bundle of letters from Mum and read many again. I found it a slightly strange experience as in some ways it was not unlike when I had first read the letter, fresh out of the letterbox. Mum's voice is strong. I hear her 'news' and thoughts and dip into her world, just as I did when she first wrote them. But my attention is piqued at mentions of her health and her feelings .... now I'm reading them for clues, not just for communication, like before. Every now and then I laugh out loud, then think with a smile about Mum's sense of humour. Once in a while there's a passage that brings tears to my eyes. Like the interment service for her friend, Hazel. The family had not wanted any flowers but Mum thought that rather bleak. She asked the family's permission to place a single rose (she chose a terracotta-coloured one) with the casket, and tried to hold back the tears as the funeral director placed it there. At least Hazel had had her flower.

Writing at this stage is also revealing strange mind tricks. Maybe because of working with this material again, Mum's death does not seem all that long ago. Then I'm faced with evidence to the contrary. Like an email from Máire, written two years ago in answer to some questions about Mum, triggered by writing about her. I'm almost surprised that it's now five years ago and many, many things have happened.

Dear Mum

My main news this week is that I have applied to do a Bachelor of Science at Wollongong University, majoring in ecology. I'm going to do it very part time: just one unit a semester to begin with. That will involve one lecture and one tutorial a week. I should be able to fit that into the juggle, I think. At that rate it could take me 12 years, but I'll probably speed up and take more on as the boys get older. Karen says one of the best things for a child's education is seeing a parent continue learning too. Peter's been talking about wanting to wind down his workload and I know I'll be feeling more pressure to earn, so I feel this will add something else to the mix. Reactions from friends have been mixed.

lots of love

Alison xxx

Dear Mum

We have a bottle of your wine to drink this year. Your drinking notes said 2007. When you died, 2007 seemed a way off. Now here it is, with little ado. Perhaps we'll drink it on your birthday. Oscar, who you didn't know, is, we have decided, a very thick cat. I'm mildly disappointed in him as I thought he was quick and smart. But his brain resembles a colander, I've decided. Things fall out of the holes. At great pains, he learnt to use the cat flap. We had a deluxe model fitted at reasonable expense in the wall by the back door (the back door being a rustic style and a shame to cut into it). He learnt very quickly to go out through it, but coming in involved stages: first, pushing through unceremoniously, then with just a little encouragement from the rear end. Then if you opened the door entirely, he'd come in, then just a little lift, then standing there calling, in sight, then calling out of sight … then he was doing it automatically. Getting to that stage took four months or so. He was doing brilliantly, casually coming in and out at his leisure, for about a fortnight … then he appeared to have forgotten entirely. Quite mysterious.

love from Alison

xxx

✢

I've become aware, writing about Mum, that it was in her early forties that, from my point of view, at least, she started to decline. I'm a very different person to her, and not inclined to follow her path ... but knowing that, and being aware of the cliché 'mid-life crisis', adds certainty to the 'extras' that I take on in my life. It's important to keep your spirits up by whatever means: swimming in my lunch hour, buying more sheet music for my tin whistle, going on camping trips with other families. Having younger children than Mum did at my age also probably makes me feel more in the full burst and stream of life. My eldest may—or may not—leave home in ten years' time. When I was at school ten years seemed an age. I suppose at one point, such a span of time represented most of my life. Now of course, while, yes, on the one hand it's a long time, I can also contemplate that it will go and before I know it, I'll be there, ten years older, with less dependent children, maybe more time. So I pick away at the guitar and start a course of study.

At times I've felt in danger of being consumed by domesticity: the drudgery involved with keeping a household together, the fragmentation that arises from a busy, bitty life tending to daily, small needs. I tend to attribute the danger of being consumed with having children—they create more mess and more work, and leave you with less time to deal with that, and less time to do the things which balance it out. But there are many other pressures which threaten to consume living souls. Work can take over ... a million things can take over. We all have our private battles in the fight to keep our spirits alive.

Every now and then an image or an idea comes into view which has helped me gain perspective over my life situation. When I watched a Tibetan documentary, *The Weeping Camel*, with my children, I was quite taken with the footage of the family dismantling their yurt home. They stripped off the fabric walls and the poles, and there, holding it all up, was a wheel. When that was removed, it all came down. That's me, I thought to myself. I might struggle with keeping a tidy house, I wish my work would earn me more, I sometimes feel I can't see much beyond my own domestic world, but for my family, I'm the wheel that holds it all together. I just keep turning. And that's all I need to do.

Mum didn't seem to care much about her family history, but I've enjoyed finding out more about the Irish in me. And there were plenty of strong-headed genes to inherit.

I've read family notes about the McGonigle uncles: my grandfather's uncles Patrick, John and Eddie. Paddy the Crank had a knack for getting cars going with the starting handle—an art known as cranking the engine. 'John the Horse' ran a pub for fifty years and operated a hackney cab service. His home was a 'haven of rest for men on the run', often an object of raids by 'Occupation authorities'. 'Eddie of the Roads' was said to be a great character with a hearty laugh. He built, say the notes, 'a wee tin house and shop near the Crooked Bridge and operated this shop till he died.'

I love the topsy-turvy story in a newspaper clipping about Mum's aunt, Margaret McGonigle, who became a nun. She cycled the 40 miles to the Franciscan Convent of Perpetual Adoration to be interviewed by the Abbess, Mother Clare Kelly, and was offered a place as a postulant. On her cycle home the next day, a bull broke out of a field. Says the paper: 'The only thing between her and the bull was her bicycle, until the timely arrival of two men in a donkey cart. They drove off the animal and saved her, if not from certain death, certainly from serious injury which could easily have put an end to her religious vocation.'

This is the nun that Sheila remembers visiting with Mum as children. She could talk to them, but not sit with them, only behind a grill. If they brought her a present, they had to put it on a turntable.

Then there's Mum's paternal grandfather, known as Grandfather James. His claim to 'fame' is that in 1927 he received in his home Eamon de Valera (later to become

President of Ireland). A few weeks later, James died, leaving two sons and a widow, Mary, who ran his drapers business until her son, Mum's dad, Seamus, opened his electrical shop there.

Mum barely mentioned her extended family, but had some old pictures nicely framed of several members. We have a family tree on my grandmother's side which focuses on the McCorrys. One group ended up in the States, and I have a photocopy of a letter to Sheila from her cousin, Eleanor Gallery McCorry. Eleanor is a name that crops up a lot on that tree. I now have Mum's picture of Eleanor Gallery, a handsome-looking woman in a smart Victorian dress with lots of ribbons and finery. She was my mother's great-grandmother. Eleanor McCorry writes of a visit to Ireland, to trace her roots. She joined Sheila, Máire and 'my' Eleanor at the Savoy Hotel in London where they had tea.

Mum's cousin, Mary Lynch, collected some family history in a book she called *Memories of Childhood in Ireland in the Thirties*. It gives a little window into another part of the family. She'd lived for a while with her grandparents at Laburnum House, Queen Street, Newry, with its laburnum tree overhanging the wall in the side garden, a Virginia creeper that covered the walls in rich red leaves, and its reassuringly solid black front door. Patrick and Ellen McDonald (my mother's maternal grandparents and my great-grandparents), like many families at the time, had fourteen children, one of them my grandmother, Sheila. When Mum's cousin Mary lived at the house, seven or eight of Patrick and Ellen's children still lived there, including Mary's aunt Ethna, a teacher who like to travel abroad, had olive skin and dark hair and eyes, said to have been inherited from the Gallery Spanish ancestors.

There was no sign of the Depression at Laburnum House, writes Mary. It was an orderly, well-kept household, occupied by busy people. Groceries were ordered by telephone ('by Aunt Mary Agnes ... I never saw my grandmother use the telephone. I think she regarded it somewhat suspiciously') and delivered weekly, sometimes by a messenger boy, sometimes by van; the fishmonger and butcher made daily deliveries, while laundry was despatched weekly. Shirts, table linen and handkerchiefs returned crisp and white from the local steam laundry by horse and cart.

Mary's notes reveal the domestic workings of the household. There was a primitive washing machine: like a small tank on legs, which was filled, emptied and operated by hand. A handle on the top was rotated till the clothes were clean enough, and after rinsing, the clothes were pressed through a mangle on the top. Fresh meat and fish were kept on shelves in the coldroom near the back door, under metal domes pierced with holes that allowed the air to circulate. Aunt Ethna used the Electrolux cylinder vacuum cleaner every Saturday morning, when she cleaned the house from top to bottom: all twelve rooms on three floors. Mary helped with dusting and polishing, shining the Jacobean oak furniture, with its intricate carvings.

When the aunts, who were 'very clothes-conscious and paid a great deal of attention to appearances', needed a special outfit, they'd take a trip to Dublin or Belfast, but otherwise, the local shop would send half a dozen dresses to the house on approval. Then there'd be much fun while trying them on.

Ellie was housekeeper and did most of the domestic chores, with some help at the weekends. Says Mary later, 'Her one blind spot was cooking.' The only time Mary remembered raised voices was over the mutton broth:

'Mutton Broth' had a decidedly adverse effect on my grandmother. She would ascend to the kitchen and declare loudly that it was too greasy, that the fat needed to be continually skimmed off the top. Now Auntie Ellie's heart was most definitely not in the cooking, besides, she would be occupied with other tasks, she would forget completely about the soup. A decided 'ticking-off' by grandmother would ensue. Auntie Ellie would shed tears, put on her coat and visit a friendly neighbour for a soothing cup of tea. After which, duly comforted, she would return. And all would be tranquil until the next time 'Mutton Broth' was on the menu.

Jam-making was a more harmonious affair. Ellen took charge, directing all hands for picking, then topping and tailing, washing, weighing. Fruit and sugar went into a large pot like a cauldron, with a blue enamel interior and a sturdy handle. Mary remembers the summer days with an aroma of boiling sugar and fruit, Grandmother Ellen in her neat apron, stirring and stirring with a long wooden spoon. Row upon row of pots would then line the cupboards: blackcurrant, gooseberry, rhubarb and ginger, marrow and ginger.

Ellen always wore black, according to Mary Lynch, with a high collar and brooch. She had a 'marvellous full-length Persian lamb coat, which she loved to wear' with her black ribbon-trimmed boater. She usually wore her very long hair in a bun held in place by tortoiseshell combs. At night, she'd let it down, and even as an old lady it reached her waist.

Ellen loved good furniture and paintings. Sounds familiar, I think. She would French-polish the tables no matter how busy she was. Patrick, on the other hand, liked books and gardening. His collection included *Butler's Lives of the*

Saints, the complete works of Dickens and H. G. Wells, Shakespeare and Sir Walter Scott.

The family was involved in the town and invitations to balls and dances stood on the mantelpiece in the dining room. Some were members of the local musical society which put on Gilbert and Sullivan shows every year: *The Gondoliers*, *Pirates of Penzance* or *The Mikado*.

Everyone cried when Isabel, the second youngest daughter, entered the community of the Sisters of the Poor Clares at an early age. 'As if she was going to the ends of the earth,' recalls Mary. The Poor Clares were strictly enclosed, and she would not be allowed to enter her own home again.

This was my mother's Auntie Isabel, who by all accounts, liked her luxuries too. Mary described her as a highly intelligent woman who made steady progress from junior teacher to headmistress; a talented musician, drama teacher and a needlewoman whose tapestries are works of art.

My great-grandmother's household sounds like one my mother might have liked: the cultured goings-on and polished furniture. There are echoes of her own tastes in the family: an aunt who loved drama and music, a grandmother who loved fine furniture and paintings; another aunt who loved gardening and listening to classical music.

The picture is one of culture and fine things, but it's not how I perceive my mother's family, when I think of visiting my own grandparents, for instance, in London. Perhaps it's just the sheen that the past takes on, that smooths over the less appealing facts, and presents a postcard view of life instead: rhythms apparent from afar—two-week holidays at the beach, returning pink-cheeked and refreshed, working week routines and weekend rhythms, polished furniture. Perhaps these sound more appealing and even exciting once concertinaed and described in print.

It's good to 'meet' Mum's ancestors. I look in the mirror in the bathroom and wonder if I resemble any of them. There is a picture of Ellen and Patrick when they're young—before the brood of fourteen. Máire used to say I looked like the Ellen in that picture, and I was very flattered, as she looks lovely. If I am like her, though, I hope I don't spread like she did later!

Among all these forebears there is more than a hint of Mum. Those headstrong men on the McGonigle side, for a start. And the McDonalds' taste for finery. I've certainly come a long way from the early days, when, months after Mum's death, I could not push my mind back much further than her Burwash years. It feels good to have stretched out her life in my mind. By stripping off the labels, I've painted a broader, fairer picture of her, and find myself liking her all the more for it.

I do feel the love for her grow as well, but I know people find it odd to talk about love for someone who's died. It's a tricky one. The person's in the past, but the feeling isn't.

Mum would have loved our final move. How we ended up buying the house next door. We really liked our little spot in Austinmer. We could walk to Thirroul, walk to Austinmer beach. We had the railway, and you couldn't deny the trains' screeching in the night, but it was true that you got used to them and after a while, simply did not hear them. The street was quiet and the boys made friends with other children and played cricket in the driveways. So when the house came up for sale next door, a year after our move out of the city, we thought we could do a lot worse.

It turned out to be quite a move, however, as the house was tenanted, and the tenants decided they'd like to take over no. 9, where we were. The real estate agent was not going to make it easy and insisted that the place be absolutely empty for them to do their inspection. So the tenants moved their stuff out of no. 11's garage, into no. 13's carport. We moved—with the help of bemused removalists—some of our things into the garage and the rest into a large tent on the front lawn, lent and put up by a generous friend. We cleaned up and the next day had our inspection. The tenants were then free to empty their house, and once done, we could move things from the tent and garage to the house!

We hung on to our house in Sydney for a little while. It was a tie to Sydney and the inner-city life there. When the time came to sell it, we decided to farewell it by staying there one last night with some old friends, who'd known us there and also lived near our new place. We descended on the place with mats and sleeping bags and filled the house one last time with our voices.

The house looked better without us. The walls were clean and bare in pale blue paint. The wooden floors were shiny and clutter free. The few architectural details—like Peter's stained glass and the pot-belly in the dining area—looked great. Without a family of four it looked like a boutique inner-city terrace, stylish and cute.

We shouted a number of friends to a meal at the local Turkish pide restaurant we'd first known as a single room with a black curtain at the counter with silvery planets and stars on it. Now it was a vast enterprise with belly dancing shows, a packed large room for eat-in customers, and a healthy takeaway business too. Little Kathleen danced with the young belly dancer, waving her hands and shaking her hips.

Back at the house I slept fairly badly. A sleeping bag on a

quilt was not much of a mattress for a wooden floor. But it was nice to soak up the atmosphere in the house. I could hear the soft breathing of my friends and family. With the soft breathing, the house itself seemed to be sighing gently. It was a swirl of faces and ghosts of voices: parties we'd had before children, dinner parties when expecting, children's birthday parties, squashed in but friendly. People visiting, popping in ... I felt like the house was saying goodbye to me almost as much as I was farewelling it. And best of all, it was a happy house, it was happy with us, happy with what we'd brought it: my waters breaking at 6 in the evening ('Oh God ... I mean, oh good,' said Peter); bringing babies home, sitting up in the night with sleepless ones, toddlers playing with water in the courtyard; flames and sizzle with vongole and spaghetti; meals around the table; tea in the morning ... running down the stairs for the phone when Mum died.

A woman I met at a friend's birthday dinner asked me what I wrote about and I told her the current project, about my mother.

'What did she die of?' she asked very directly.

'Dilated cardiomyopathy because of alcohol,' I replied, equally directly.

'Was she always an alcoholic?' she asked.

I shuddered internally at the 'alcoholic' label: 'No, from around forty, I think.'

'Why did she do that?' she asked, as if there were a simple answer.

I shrugged my shoulders. 'I guess I'll never really know ... a bad coping mechanism, I suppose ... at some point she found it was some sort of escape.'

'That's what I mean, what was she escaping from?'

I have no answer, but part of me wants to say, 'Life. It can be tough. We have expectations, responsibilities, disappointments and sometimes we don't deal with them well. It's not a series of flash cards to which we respond simplistically. A nuance in a relationship might push us one way or another; an opportunity might save us from a destructive path; a slight change of thinking can alter our whole outlook on life. It takes an effort to engage and keep living to the full. There's no doubt that it's worth the effort, but not everyone manages and it's naive to think they will.'

In the very last stages of writing this, just a day or so before finalising the manuscript, when my head had been filled with thoughts of Mum and my childhood, I took Harry to band practice in the morning before school. As we waited to turn into the main road, I noticed a large fishing boat quite close to shore. Then I saw a big splash. 'Did you see that? Do you think it might be … '

Instead of turning right, we continued over the main road and parked the car. There was the splash again—and a large flipper of a whale. 'Wow! Look at that!' And again, and again. It was so lovely to see. So exciting to think of these magnificent creatures in our ocean.

The whale was heading further out to sea, so we got in the car and I drove Harry to school. He turned on the radio. It was tuned to the only station we could get that morning in the shadow of the escarpment. Cliff Richard was singing 'The Young Ones'. I explained who he was. 'He's even a "Sir" now.' After dropping Felix off a bit later, I got back in the car and started the engine. The radio started up with 'Time to Say Goodbye', the music that had played at Mum's funeral. I'd only ever heard it on the CD and at the funeral. It was a shock. I could hardly believe it. I was heading home to finish writing a passage about her life. I was nearing the end of this prolonged writing episode. It started to rain and, as I flicked on the windscreen wipers, tears rolled up out of nowhere.

SIX

VILLAGE LIFE

Writing to me in Paris, sometimes my mother's letters seemed more full of my dad's activities than her own. A crisis was looming, but what would emerge the other side was not all bad.

After years abroad, Mum was back to the greenery of England and a quiet life in Hawkhurst. Back to English weather, with its sleet, rain and occasional 'big freeze', like the one where they were snowed in for two days, and Dad tried to walk to the station, only to find that trains were only going as far as Tunbridge Wells, not to London where he worked, so he had to walk back, a round trip of 2.5 hours.

By now my sister was looking, and soon finding, work in London, living for a little while in one of the flats which I'd shared with some medical students. I was in my third year of my law degree and was completing the second half—two years in Paris.

To be honest, there was so much coming and going, Mum and Dad moving between Houston, Egypt and England, then me between England and Paris, I find it hard to pinpoint exactly where we all were at various times. Was I in Paris and they still in Houston? Or was I in London and they back? Perhaps I could be a sleuth and go back to letters and scrutinise the postmarks and addresses.

In any case, when I moved to Paris, Mum and Dad took me. We drove a packed car over, taking the ferry, I think, then spending a few days in the north of France, staying, the three of us, in a series of stunning hotels that were part of the Relais & Châteaux organisation that combined gourmet restaurants with excellent accommodation, in medieval castles and the like. The landscape was flat; you'd be forgiven for describing it as bleak, but I remember one hotel in particular that was built in ancient blue-grey stone. The dining room had enormous heavy chairs, candles on the table, beautiful wine and exquisite food. Mum loved it. So did I. When we found the hall of residence in Paris, I was not so impressed. There was a sign asking for quiet. My tiny room, barely any bigger than a single bed, was grimy. Its tinier-still washbasin area took me a day to clean. Mum and Dad stayed just a night or so in Paris. They'd thought of staying longer, but Dad found the parking a nightmare and they decided to head home.

With me in Paris, in my grotty hall of residence, Dad back at work in London, and Mum a little too much by herself in a house surrounded by rabbit-run fields, letters continued between us all. Mum got a dog, the cocker spaniel she called Daisy, who she really loved and who became the main focus of her life. She reported in one letter that Daisy had been in the wars. While walking in Bedgebury Forest, she'd jumped a fence that was topped with barbed wire. Dad thought she'd just brushed it and since he couldn't see any blood, thought she was okay. But back at the house, they both checked her and found she had a really bad cut.

I phoned the vet to say we'd be bringing her up as it needed stitches. They had a look and said that it did need stitching but as they use a general anaesthetic with stitching, they would use the new method of stapling! They gave her an injection to sedate her and we sat in the waiting room till all the patients had been seen.

Little Daisy was quite woozy by the time her turn came and they put her on the 'operating table'. Mum held her back legs apart to expose the cut and Dad had her front legs. The nurse got ready to shave around the wound and Nick, the vet, decided he had to take photos of the procedure for a lecture he was giving soon. ' "My hands will be famous," chipped in the nurse, " ... will we get royalties?" Nick started stapling and Dad said, "I think I'll ... " and slid gracefully to the floor in a dead faint!'

Unperturbed, the vet dragged my father by the shoulders into the middle of the room, leaving him to recover there while another nurse took over the front legs. Daisy had about fourteen staples, during which time Dad came round and took up position on a chair, looking very grey.

Mum's life was very quiet at this stage. My sister and I were further afield, Dad was out of the house for a very long day and would also go away for days at a time for business. But when she had the chance she enjoyed dressing up for company dos—particularly if they were picked up by a car and driver. Dad's job meant invitations to the opera, Wimbledon, theatre, dances at top hotels and the like. They saw all the major shows, including *Phantom of the Opera* twice.

When once they were invited to the Last Night at the Proms, a car came for them in Kent, dropping them for a pre-concert drink. They were thrilled with their second-row seats and dinner at Silks afterwards, and amused to find they featured quite a bit in the TV recording, which they watched the next day. 'I watched it as I did the ironing and after a while I had worked out where we had been sitting. Suddenly there we were!' Mum wrote to me.

They joined the Lansdowne Club just off Berkeley Square in London after I'd had an evening job there as 'cocktail assistant' in the bar in my second year of law at Kings College. It was a rather eccentric place, typically English. Tea was served in the ballroom by a sometimes scary woman called Kitty. The tall, quiet man who washed up in the kitchen slept on the streets, it was said. The snack bar downstairs by the pool was run by an Eastern European, Polish or Hungarian? who'd escaped and gone to clown school. She was high-spirited, read tarot cards and lived in Chelsea in a flat furnished entirely from items found on the street. The customers were equally odd. One, a tall lanky Lord, used to ask every night without fail for a 'glass of red wine and a bowl of crisps, please.' Then he'd proceed to sit at a small round table and chatter—by himself. He was quite normal compared to another man, in a good, up-to-date suit, who appeared to be talking to someone at his side who was not there. When you came up to him to ask what he'd like, he'd snap out of his 'conversation' and give you an order, appearing quite okay. Mum and Dad had visited me there a couple of times. When they learnt how cheap the rooms were, they were keen to join. You need to be proposed by two members. I organised that for them. One of the proposers might have been the man who liked to chat to me in the bar; he was a tailor to the queen, no less.

> We went up to London yesterday and stayed at the club—in the same room as last week, 105. We went to a dinner dance at the Marriott and it was very good. The cabaret had dancers, a comedian, acrobats and Sacha Distel. We met three couples who'd we'd been on shoots with.

They even had an invite to Buckingham Palace, to one of the big garden parties that the Queen holds for the civilians.

> We had our invitation to the Palace last week. It's quite funny—we have a big white card saying 'The Lord Chamberlain is commanded by Her Majesty the Queen to invite Mr and Mrs Michael Haynes ... to ...' Then we have three separate yellow cards that we have to hand in and a sticker for the car. I'll have to buy a hat next week.

That was a busy week: *Aïda* one night, ladies' finals at

Wimbledon another, and garden party at Buckingham Palace on Wednesday.

But generally, life was quiet and Mum's orbit small. Perhaps it even began to shrink. She wrote to me about saving magazines for Sheila, and passing on cat food tins after Blackie, aged sixteen, was buried under the lawn. Dad's interests continued to take him outdoors, while Mum carried on with needlework, reporting doing so much one week that her thumb was sore from rubbing on the canvas, so she'd got herself a thumb stall with an elastic around the wrist, and cut the top off so she could grip the needle. 'Quite a clever idea don't you think?'

She liked to organise minor projects in the house: the plumber to fit a new shower, the cabinet maker to make a new leaf for the dining room table and repolish the top; getting a cushion recovered for the guest room; repairing the bird table; hunting for old pine furniture for one of the rooms.

Mum and Dad took a holiday in Sicily, staying in Taormina, a very beautiful town with a tree-lined high street and a Roman amphitheatre up on the hill. I spent two summers in Sicily as an au pair. They'd liked the sound of Sicily, with its rich history of invasions (it was in Palermo, its capital, that I'd seen Arab Norman churches). I'd travelled a little while there and they'd asked me which towns I thought they'd like.

One of the few photographs that Mum kept showed her on the way up to Mount Etna, grey ash behind her, her head covered in a headscarf against the wind.

Mum wasn't 'horsey' but she would help out every now and then. If Dad went away for a while he usually arranged for someone to deal with the horse, but once when the help forgot, it was Mum who did the feed, topped up the hay, filled up the water bucket and put the horse in the stable.

After a few years, Dad's job took him back to Houston but Mum elected to stay in Kent and visit every few months. She was very fond of Daisy and said she didn't want to leave her. Knowing how dreadful the place had been for her, I can't say I blamed her. Some people saw it as her putting the dog before my father. When I look at it, the job came first. The hole in Dad's life gaped larger, and in Mum's too. While she claimed to like living on her own in Hawkhurst, it was a lonely spot. I wouldn't say she moped, because she never said anything was wrong, but she certainly slowed right down.

Mum helped Dad find furniture in the States to replace the initial rented stuff, things that would also fit in back home. 'It was quite difficult as either everything was too big, too flashy or the wrong colours,' she told me. While she stayed for a couple of weeks, she did the 'usual chores, a bit of needlework, reading and a bit of television.'

The suburb was a little more upmarket than the one they'd lived in previously. 'The reason I think this is because there's not a soul around during the week. Everybody seems to be out at work to cover the cost of the house and at weekends we see the occasional person mowing the front lawn and they do wave but that's it. No children anywhere and therefore no noise.' It sounded deadly.

In England, Mum bought herself a copy of Delia Smith's *Cooking for One* and tried a few recipes. The birds got leftovers and the ones that didn't meet with approval. She'd take Daisy out each morning, perhaps around Bewlbridge Reservoir, a man-made lake surrounded by grass and trees, 'Then there's a trip to Cranbrook for something or other.' She went to auction viewings in Battle and Cranbrook. Most weeks she met another friend with a dog for a walk. 'I see a friend Mari for coffee every few months.' And she had her history class. The seventeenth-century house and what there was to learn from writers of the time, London cemeteries. She wrote to Dad once a week and included cuttings from the papers.

When Dad returned a second time from Houston, they toyed with the idea of moving, looking at houses that would give him half an hour's less travel, as his office had moved. But nothing quite right came up.

For me, decades later writing this, the years are all

blurring. My parents are moving backwards and forwards between Houston and England. There's the occasional event or holiday that is hard to place in the chronology. I too am on the move. I spent two years in Paris, then went to Australia for a working holiday. University had not been a happy time for me. I loved Paris but I didn't like the university. Law felt very rigid and restrictive; I felt that if I worked in it, I'd be flitting between a psychoanalyst and Weight Watchers for the rest of my life. I even decided not to sit the last couple of exams, thinking instead I'd revise for them over the summer holidays and do re-sits in a calm fashion. 'Your father is very angry. He says you're to come home and study for the exams,' my mother told me. Well, I wasn't going to. I went to live with my aunt Sheila over the summer, got a job in an insurance company in the City, passed my exams in September then in October 1987, just after the great storm in England's south-east, I went to Australia for a year. I was back a year later, and in 1990 emigrated to live with Peter. We married in 1991.

It was not many years after returning from Houston that Dad took early retirement. He was at home more with Mum and—only they know the details—by the mid-nineties their differences were brought to a head. Mum's world had started to narrow. She became less enthusiastic about having people round for dinner like they'd done before, and less willing to venture out on trains and even in the car to family or other events around the country. Her problem drinking persisted. Feeling he could not take things anymore, Dad left her. He'd met someone else, through a swimming club reunion. I'd been living in Australia for a few years then, and learnt about it all from a distance.

What had happened to Mum? It seems like something died in her. That she gave up in some way. She closed down and lost spirit. When a parent has been in a marriage all your life, it's hard to step back and say what happened. Not that, quite frankly, I feel it would be right to examine my parents' marriage publicly. Mum was a nicer person to be with when her interests drew her outwards. But for a while, she seemed to withdraw. It had been, no doubt, a gradual process. In fact, Mum once told me things had not been right since my sister was born—and that was thirty-two years before. It's hard to be more precise. I'd been in Australia for a few years when the split came. I wasn't that surprised—which I suppose reveals my understanding of the situation.

No one blamed Dad for leaving Mum; many were not surprised. They appeared to have little in common and had been doing less and less together over the years. There was little sense of togetherness. I was pleased for him in many ways, as I was glad he could have the comfort of a fuller relationship. I was sad for their partnership, however, and sad for Mum.

She took the separation very badly. She was bitter and perhaps even desperate at first. Her feelings of status were so wrapped up in her marriage. She was stung at the indignity, yet had done little to try and save the situation before it was too late. The companionship and comfort had worn thin. The love was still there on both sides ('She was just a girl when I met her,' Dad told me later) but it was just not feasible anymore.

Dad had moved out and wanted to sell the house. But Mum decided she'd stay put. Then out of the blue she decided she'd like to move after all and would take the pick of the furniture. She and Dad separated judicially—not a divorce, so they were still married at the time of her death. She found an old house in a village about twenty minutes' drive away. It was a section of a big old sixteenth-century building, Swan Inn. The house she was buying was called Cygnet Cottage. She'd always wanted a period home. She finally got one. It had beams at the front, leadlight windows. A winding staircase up to the third floor. A small courtyard garden that suited her, if not Daisy.

Once the papers were signed, all her energy went on planning ahead where every bit of furniture would go, working out what curtains she'd need, where the pictures would go and whether she needed new lampshades. She didn't want to wait till she was there, she wanted to work it all out before she moved the furniture.

The cottage had two small bedrooms on a third floor, two good-sized rooms one level down, one she used as her bedroom, facing the high street, and the other one she used as a sitting room. It had a big built-in cupboard where she stored her needlework and she soon had a gas heater fitted in a fireplace. Downstairs was a large, handsome living room with a giant inglenook fireplace, and a small kitchen to the front. There was a cellar too, where she could store extra kitchenware.

Just before she moved, when I asked if she was getting out more, she replied, 'In fact I'm going out even less! I went to the hairdressers last Friday for the first time in about five weeks and I haven't taken Daisy out at all. I just don't feel like it.' She was going through the motions, but life was flat.

Moving house gave her something to focus on. She crammed every piece of furniture that she possibly could into the house. It was hard to move around in some rooms! Dad helped her for quite a while, fixing up things she needed. But she couldn't help her bitterness, and one sour word too many and he didn't go back. He never saw her again until that day driving through the village several years later with me.

She was brave for a while, and set up the home. Spent days sorting, clearing, dusting, vacuuming, walking Daisy and going back to Kent for bits and pieces. Máire and John helped her unpack. She stood there in a pink angora sweater and beads, surrounded by boxes. After thirty-three years of marriage, she really was on her own.

The village consisted of several fine old pubs, a high street with tile-fronted houses, a small supermarket and a few other shops. It was ideal. The post office was a 'wonderful village one', so small only six people could stand in it. 'They are so nice, they take your letter and they stick on the stamps.'

She wasn't eating well and news filtered out about artery problems in her legs. Her legs puffed up and she seemed to have difficulty walking. Not long after came the crisis, where she was taken to hospital and stayed a month. She almost died. The doctors told my aunts and sister later that they'd hardly expected her to make it the weekend. But she did survive. And gradually her health improved—with a battery of drugs.

Perhaps the way she didn't eat was a so-called cry for help. But if it was, it backfired on her. It was the final blow to her already weakened system. More than a decade of too much white wine, and no doubt not enough food to balance it out, had wreaked havoc on her heart. She could never have guessed the damage she'd done to herself.

Sheila and Máire rallied round. Mum had always been the capable one. With the good school, the ambitious husband, the nice home ... now she was the single woman with a heart problem. They'd known nothing of her drinking problems but now it made sense of some odd phone conversations they'd had over the years.

Fiona spent weeks travelling up and down from Devon helping Mum. She found her skirts with big waists from charity shops as until the diuretics kicked in, Mum's swollen waist (along with legs and ankles) meant she needed skirts several sizes bigger than usual.

Dad and Fiona kept me in touch with faxes and phone calls mainly. Sheila wrote. I was on tenterhooks, wondering just how bad she was and whether—or when—I should fly over.

When she came back out of hospital she had to struggle to climb the stairs to her bedroom. It hurt and she became breathless. After a while she improved, did leg exercises as prescribed by the physiotherapist. But she could still barely walk down the high street to the bank, or the grocers. It was months, too, before she was strong enough to drive.

'I'm trying to get back to normal,' she wrote to me in Australia. 'But struggling at times.' When she did start driving, a half-hour drive to Tesco at Hastings tired her out to such a degree she spent the next two days in bed. 'I find this is what I have to do, but it's a start.' She tried to get out once a week, although it was tough on her breathing.

When she got pneumonia and pleurisy the winter after her hospital stint, Sheila called her every day and reported she sounded stronger each time. Sheila wrote one month:

No doubt you heard about the day last week when I phoned Fiona to report that Eleanor's line was constantly engaged. To cut a long story short Fiona contacted the surgery and they in turn contacted the police. It all sounds very dramatic but we knew the phone was off the hook but did not know if she was OK. When the two policemen went into the room she was sitting in bed doing her needlework. Luckily she saw the funny side of it and did not connect me phoning Fiona and thought that the surgery wanted to contact her. Some documents had dislodged the handset. When I phoned her that evening she said, 'You do not know what kind of a day I have had.' I played it down, but little does she realise how upset and worried we all were.

Early on after the crisis, the specialist told her she'd need a heart transplant if she were to survive longer than a year. He asked her what she thought about that and she said 'fine'. It would involve tissue tests at Harefield and various other tests before being put on a waiting list. While a new heart could give a patient another ten years, there were issues of rejection and infection. Being thin, she needed a small heart. Not everyone on a waiting list lasted until a heart became available.

In Australia, I tried to find out about heart transplants and what was involved. I called St Vincent's Hospital and they said if I came in, someone would talk to me. They did—in a public waiting room. It was not exactly the private, comforting chat I had envisaged. I left, I think with a brochure and the feeling that Mum would be lucky to find a heart in time.

She had various scans which made her feel she was getting closer to the transplant and she told me she sometimes thought about how there was someone 'walking around with my heart.' Drugs helped her eat again, and the breathing started to improve and her colour picked up: 'I no longer have a blue face and hands.'

Mum's new neighbours in the village seemed caring. The rector, Roy, called round. The congregation routinely prayed for the sick, and Jean, the elderly neighbour opposite, felt Mum might like to thank him. 'He's very nice and I used to see him a lot when I was walking Daisy. He stayed for 1.5 hours. I kept trying not to yawn but I felt quite tired.'

Once her strength picked up, however, she could get out a little. 'It was so nice walking down the high street. I met three people that I know.'

She had a little courtyard garden that she planted up:

My little garden is looking pretty. The bluebells are out, purple osteospermums and white geraniums. My sweet pea is climbing happily up its wigwam and will be a very pale pink when it flowers. My chive flowers are out so it's looking quite colourful.

In the spring the crocus and snowdrops pushed through, followed a little later by daffodils. Soon she had a burgeoning herb garden: basil, dill, coriander, chives, sage, rosemary, parsley and mint, protected from the slugs by gravel.

She wrote about the 'wildlife' that visited the garden. Sitting in the lounge one afternoon a bird landed at her feet. 'How sweet, I thought and looked down and it was a frog!

My legs shot into the air faster than I thought they could move! I banged my book against the chair and he hopped away. I couldn't relax after that—I kept looking for him but didn't see him eventually go. Then one morning I was watering the wall pots and saw what I thought was a big bumblebee on a flower. It was a tiny bat.'

She had very soon made friends with Jean Maude Roxby, who lived in a beautiful old house opposite. Jean was in her eighties and quite a character. She had studied sculpture at the Chelsea School of Art and was proud to have had Henry Moore as tutor once. She had known Rudyard Kipling as a child when he lived in Bateman's, now a National Trust property a few miles out of the village. Jean lived next door to her sister-in-law.

Mum would cook them something like a casserole, which she knew they wouldn't do for themselves. Or she might have them over for coffee. 'Jean was very quiet and at one stage I'm sure she was asleep! Perhaps the heat is too much for her and she is 82,' she said after one visit.

Jean invited her over for a drink on Easter Sunday. A glass of wine, Twiglets and crisps were the usual fare. Another time they both went to a neighbour's, but, said Mum, 'The conversation was a bit odd as Jean is very deaf. She would mishear a word and the entire conversation would go off on a different angle.'

One day there were some people outside Cygnet Cottage. In this stage of Mum's life she was quite outgoing. She had to be. The institutional props of marriage were no longer in place, and faced with what an insular life could do to you, she'd turned her view outwards again. So, seeing they had an interest in the cottage, it was natural she should strike up a conversation. It turned out they'd lived in the house in the 1940s, so she invited them in.

The man's parents had lived there and next door—which at the time had been one larger house—with four children. Mum's cloakroom had been an outside loo, the big sitting room had been a bathroom, with the basin in the inglenook and stairs going up. The kitchen had been the father's study and the top rooms attic rooms. Next door, the big bedroom had been his grandmother's (who complained about a ghost—a woman who came out of a cupboard and wandered around the room. The vicar had come to exorcise it, with no success). When they lived there, instead of garages at the back, there was a blacksmith's shop. 'All this because I said hello,' said Mum, pleased with herself, and tickled pink at the extra information.

Mum was friendly to villagers and to new people she met, but she'd cut off most people she'd known before her marriage split, using a disagreement as an excuse, or an embarrassing scene, or simply not returning phone calls or following up.

But she was pleased when Fiona made the journey up and came to visit, and she saw her sisters a few times a year. I thought of the small group that she still allowed close as her 'inner circle': my sister, me, Sheila, Máire and John. She introduced them to Jean across the road when Sheila had bought a book of poems by Rudyard Kipling and wanted Jean to write a few words in it as she'd known Kipling. She arranged to take them all over for a drink, taking everything with her, including nibbles.

At first Mum paid a local pensioner to shop for her, but she was not too put out when about a year later, she had to take up her own shopping again. By that time she was stronger, able to drive, although she did find the trolleys heavy, but could arrange home delivery to avoid having to push it too far.

Her health was far from good, but village life suited her. 'It's interesting,' she wrote, 'I feel that I've really settled in to the village. Every time I go down the high street I meet people who chat and ask how I'm doing. It's nice.'

She went to a history class once a week and researched in her many books in between, writing up notes—with photocopied pictures as illustrations. It might be Ham House or glass in the seventeenth century or Stuart costume. She couldn't manage the day trips but would plan her essays and visit Heathfield where she could get colour photocopies for her notes. 'I think I'll write an essay on men's hairstyles and headgear in the Georgian era. It's such a long period, 1714–1830.'

She got to know her neighbours, and revelled in the fact that one of them was a Lord. They'd borrow books, give a bag of tomatoes from the greenhouse, drop round a bunch of flowers from the garden; pop in a bar of chocolate to say thank you for watering courgettes and beans.

When the history class had a visitor talking about Rudyard Kipling, Jean gave Mum a few postcards she and her brothers received from him as children, some gifts from Egypt and the *Just So Stories* signed for Jean. She had had a heavy cold and wrote, 'I don't feel like going to class but with such treasures I'll have to.'

When the history class a half-hour drive away was to be moved further away, Mum got one started in the village instead. It was quite a performance, going through Sussex University, arranging to use the village hall. She put lots of posters up and approached a teacher and the university. It was up to her to employ the teacher and hire the hall. They were oversubscribed. I heard all about the plans in her regular letters. She sent me a poster too, so I could see what a good job she'd done. Soon after this session started, the newcomers said how professional it was. 'I told them that it ought to be as our teacher was a university and National Trust lecturer.'

She got quite excited when someone phoned asking about the history class. Mum suggested she look at some of her work and lent her a book. She was keen. The history teacher was encouraging too: ' ... although it's very nice for her to have knowledgeable people ... it's really nice to have someone who is really "raw".'

She catered for the tea break, 'negotiating' cupboard space in the hall kitchen for tea, coffee, sugar and biscuits.

Sometimes she went to NADFAS (National Association of Decorative and Fine Arts Societies) lectures on, for instance, old English spoons: 'the speaker was Ian Pickford who is well known from the Antiques Roadshow on TV. It did me good to have an outing. I got out a dress that I hadn't worn for years and one of my smart bags.'

She was more able than some of her new friends, and found herself helping out a lot. She took her elderly friend Clare to the dentist in Heathfield one June day when it was a sweltering 80 degrees, the hottest day of the year.

She often did shopping errands for her older friends. She picked up Vaseline or pale pink nail polish for someone at the chemist. 'It's very difficult shopping for her because she gets things muddled up but the things I get are OK in the end.' Clare called one Sunday afternoon, the day after Mum's last birthday, to ask her to take her to casualty as she'd fallen down some stairs, skinned her elbow and hurt her back. She picked Clare up at 3.15 (she'd looked very shaken, Mum said) and finally left casualty at 9 pm—driving back in the pitch dark with heavy rain and fog to boot. 'I got in at 9.30, absolutely shattered.'

When a neighbour went into hospital with cancer, she went to see her every week. 'She's going downhill slowly but surely. She's walking with a Zimmer frame and is very stooped.' She took Clare and Peppie (the dog) too, 'She enjoyed seeing Clare, a fresh face … Last time I had to paint her toe nails for her! I don't mind, I just take things and her bossing in my stride.'

People often came to her with unfinished tapestry pieces, begging a favour. She'd complain and wonder how they had the nerve, but end up doing it anyway. She had a steady hand and a patient attitude. Her stitches were even and the overall effect always smooth. She continued with her tapestries, making cushion covers and samplers that would be framed and hung. The odd-job man asked her to do some cross-stitch Father Christmases for his daughter, who collected them. 'So yes, I had to do it … it took me a week to do and I have to say I made a good job of it.' (A few days later, there was a knock at the door and the girl standing there with a tub of raspberries and one of strawberries: 'for you and very many thanks.')

The neighbour's cat, called, like her grandson, Harry, thought her place was a second home and liked to sit on her knee (on a towel if she was wearing white), whether she was trying to write a letter or get on with needlework.

She lived well but was careful with her money. 'All my bills seem to go up, mind you I am in credit with some, but my monthly allowance is still the same. It might be just as well if I'm not around in a few years—I wouldn't be able to live!' she exaggerated.

She wrote about changes in the village: the DIY shop was closing and there would be two houses built in its place; the 'little bank' was to close, leaving the nearest one at Heathfield, a twenty-minute drive away; the post office was up for sale.

There were projects on the house, some more urgent than others. Window frames that needed painting or fixing up because they were wobbly; clippers and secateurs to have sharpened; an expensive new curtain rail to hang her coats on in the landing ('It cost £99.50. I must be mad but it is just right for the house. I ordered it when I came back from the specialist and knew I'd be around a bit longer'); a toilet bowl she decided needed turning at right angles—then she decided she could get the washing machine in the downstairs loo, getting it out of the kitchen where she never liked it being. 'The plumbing in the cloakroom looks v messy so if the measurements work out I'll be talking a lot of money but it would be worth it.'

When the builder and plumber checked out her plans, 'They looked at it and what I wanted in disbelief!! Then I explained my plan and after much measuring and discussion, lifting a man-hole cover, flushing loos etc. they decided it could be done!!! I'm now waiting for the estimate which will be high. Just hope I can afford it after all this!'

She planned a holiday in Italy. She picked the lake and the trips she might be able to do. She never made that trip but she did get to Rye the year I was there. She'd said she'd be away but was unwilling to reveal what she was doing. Afterwards she'd explained she stayed in the Mermaid Inn, as a treat. I think she got fed up with the way when you're sick you end up explaining all the time what you're up to.

Mum had drinks parties and invited neighbours, especially new ones. She had champagne delivered in boxes and would plan the canapés (stuffed cherry tomatoes, stuffed mange tout, filled tiny pastry cases and hot artichoke hearts were favourites), trying new ones most times. She would pace herself, probably getting ready the day before, maybe setting a table, or preparing plates of food. She'd 'get straight' the day after. A Sunday lunch invitation might mean shopping Thursday, setting the table Friday and getting dishes out, some of the cooking on Saturday. She'd clear up on Monday and would still be feeling tired on Tuesday.

She arranged a Dickens evening as a birthday surprise for Jean. Gerald Dickens, the great-great-grandson of Charles Dickens, lived in the village and used to tour with a one-man show, donning a frock coat and cravat and carrying a Gladstone bag. Jean was entertained and touched.

Mum enjoyed television. Watched cooking shows, BBC adaptations of the classics and the like. Wimbledon was a top attraction, writing one year, 'They have added drama as the top floor of a block of flats right next door is on fire and they've had smoke and flames billowing out. They've evacuated the picnic area and one court because of the smoke but it's under control and a police helicopter is patrolling the area.' When she wanted to watch a program on Schumann, but needed to cook lunch too, she decided it was time to buy a set for the kitchen, and spent a bit extra on a white one which would look better. 'I thought about the cost ... but decided that since I never go to the cinema or eat out a lot I deserved it!'

She'd report on new villagers: 'The new people moved into the A's house last weekend. He's a stock broker in London and is a typical "yuppie". I saw him the other morning wearing a nice green and white striped shirt, dark trousers, yellow patterned braces and yellow socks.'

When she had to wait a long time at the doctor's surgery to have a burst blood vessel in her eye looked at she was interested to note that the cleaner was the lollipop lady. (Jackie, the home help, told her how she'd seen the receptionist and she'd told her that 'this lady came in with a funny eye and it was really horrible.' There were no secrets in that village.)

Despite not really eating enough, for a spell at least, food featured strongly in her letters and phone calls. During these years when I visited annually, she always made a nice meal and, when it was more than just popping through at lunchtime, would select a good bottle of red for Peter. There were trips to Tesco where she might buy skate wings or prepared squid. Every now and then a freezerload of food needed cooking up because of a power cut or finding the door had been open for a while: one stint was five salmon fillets, four cod fillets and thirty-two giant tiger prawns. Duck breasts went in the fridge but tuna, swordfish, skate, smoked haddock, minced beef, ice cream, six soups and chicken stock had to go. The birds got bread: pita, baguette, ciabatta and pizza bases.

Her friend Hazel had recommended the free-range eggs sold at the garage and she took to them: huge, cheaper than Tesco, fresh every week and salmonella-tested. She sometimes bought a few pounds of pork sausage meat to make patties with onion, mustard, fresh sage and oregano, for the freezer. If a friend came for lunch, she might cook a pork hot-pot, which he wouldn't do for himself. (Tender as it was three hours in the oven with the lid on, and a further hour with the lid off to crisp the potatoes.)

Trips to Tunbridge Wells were fairly major. She might go in for some white sandals to go with a new dress. 'I checked Fenwick, Hobbs, Clarks Dolcis and M&S, just looking at shoes, but nothing.' That reminds me of her similar, disappointing shopping expedition in Houston, and further back, of our own search for shoes as children. She indulged us, I think now, as we often went to several towns before finding ones we liked.

If there were bargains to be had, she might venture further afield. Like the time she noticed a Sainsbury's ad for the St Leonards store for half-price champagne on Easter Saturday. They opened at 7.30 am and she was there at 7.40. 'I was awake and decided to have my pills and go. It was a very scenic trip—the primroses and bluebells were out and I had to slow down for 2 ducks crossing the road, a rabbit and a squirrel.'

Her letters were so much more full of life now that she was in Burwash on her own. During that sad phase in Hawkhurst, when she spent far too much time alone, she always found something to write about, but the action was often in my father's activities rather than her own. They lacked the zest she now revealed.

In the winter, she told me, she preferred to pick a nice day and avoid the lanes. 'They grit the main road but you never know what the lanes are like.' Some neighbours had skidded on the ice, circled, hit a tree and smashed in all the back and back window of the car.

There was fish and chips from the van every Wednesday. She was slightly put out once to be invited to supper with some neighbours, she took a very good bottle of red for them and a white for herself, as they only had oaky chardonnay which she didn't like, only to find they were buying their own dinner from the fish and chip van. 'It was nice but very expensive for me as the wine cost £6.50! Never mind, I'll learn.'

She made up by not taking wine the next time she was invited for Sunday lunch: 'her usual, everything cooked the day before and reheated in the microwave. It's just not the same as crispy roast potatoes and vegetables.'

When her good friend Hazel died of cancer, it was not a good week. 'On Monday I learnt that Hazel had died and spent most of it in tears.' Hazel's husband told her that Hazel had really enjoyed seeing her only ten days before and that she'd brought humour and contact. Hazel had been working on a needlepoint cushion and had asked him to give it to Mum to finish. Although it was a 'strictly private' funeral, Mum was invited to go. There were only eleven people and just a few prayers were said and two hymns. It was all over and done in twenty minutes then the coffin left for the crematorium. 'It all seemed so stark … nobody went to the crematorium.'

She did a bit of the needlework when she could face it. Hazel hadn't been using the same colours as the picture and seemed to be missing a hank of wool. She'd got the kit from a local woman who ran classes and when Mum wanted to ask her what colour to use, she told her she could come to a class to 'sort it out'. 'So I can't get on with it until I've been to and paid for a class. Honestly!' Later she wrote how she'd been working non-stop to get it finished. It had a complicated border that seemed to take forever.

Mum wrote telling me how she sold forty-seven books of raffle tickets in aid of the village hall to visitors who came for a coffee, and knocking on the door of 'anyone I knew.' Only one person said no. She made cakes for the village fete, for the Friends of Burwash stall: ' … chocolate brownies. Anything with chocolate sells well.' The actress Carmen Silvera, from *'Allo 'Allo*, opened the village fair one year. 'I can hear them putting up the stalls in the recreation ground,' Mum wrote. 'I'll stroll down and have a look at the stalls. The exercise will do me good. I feel very sluggish these days. I miss my walks with Daisy. They kept me very fit.' Later she reported that she'd seen the actress in a cream silky suit, a big hat and wellingtons. (It had poured with rain all morning.)

Life was busy in a gentle sort of way. 'I found I'd triple booked myself this AM!' she wrote: an appointment with the nurse, gas man doing a service and a hair appointment.

Often, she mentioned her health in the context of visiting nurses, doctors' appointments but occasionally would write, 'Not feeling too good these days. Have missed class the last 2 weeks. Perhaps I'll improve—hope so, in time for your visit.'

She wasn't too impressed with one of the doctors she saw, and was glad when she switched to another. She described a meeting she had with the one she didn't like:

He flicked through her notes.

Doctor. 'Are you well?'

Mum: 'I wouldn't say well, exactly but a lot better thanks to Dr S. putting me on Digoxin and aspirin. When I first saw Dr S. he gave me a year unless I got a transplant.'

The doctor looked up, interested.

Doctor: 'How did you get on at Harefield?'

Mum: 'I had the first test for a transplant but had improved enough not to need it.'

'With my notes sitting on his desk it all seemed so useless. Then he asked his one and only question—"How tall are you?" I wanted to say 7' 6", but decided not to be sarcastic. [She was 5' 3".] It must have been the only thing not on my notes.'

A couple of years after the crisis, and the diagnosis of cardiomyopathy, she managed to be squeezed into her specialist's last day before he took up a job in another, far-off hospital. Her heart was still enlarged, he told her, but looking better. The normal pumping level was 60, he said, hers had been 25 and was now 46. 'He shook my hand and wished me good luck. He's so nice—shame I'm losing him.'

One January, soon after New Year, she wrote telling of the dreadful weather: gales and lashing rain. The wind woke her at 1.50 am rapping the Christmas wreath on the front door against the door knocker it was tied to. Then the drainpipe outside her bedroom window rattled. By three in the morning the rain was lashing against the windows so she got up for a towel to put on the sill by the leaky window.

Then there was the total eclipse of the sun, due to occur mid-morning one August. She was up to date with what was in the media, it was talked up, and she took great interest.

The eclipse was amazing yesterday. It was quite funny because the BBC had set up facilities in Cornwall and it was raining with thick cloud. They couldn't really see anything but had it on TV via a Hercules plane. They did get total darkness and St Michael's Mount looked spectacular. Here, we had clear skies and I was able to watch the 'bite' out of the sun extending with the use of some welders' goggles which Tony had lent me. We had the drop in temperature and a look of dusk. I saw about 95% of the sun covered. Later I was speaking to the butchers and they'd been watching it from outside the forge with welders' goggles. They said the birds did go up to roost in the trees. An interesting day.

One of her new friends was a young lad who worked in one of the village shops. When his Japanese pen pal stayed, he'd booked her into the Rose & Crown at £40 (half his week's wages), as the bed & breakfasts were full. That meant he had no money left to take her out to supper. 'So of course, I had to say "you'd better bring her here for supper." He said he couldn't possibly do that and off he went, to my relief! On Sat. morning he turned up with a belated b'day card and an origami flower as he hadn't got any money to buy me a present. Then he said that "they would love to come to tea." '

She planned dinner, set the table and shopped. He was vegetarian, but wouldn't eat salads and ate only eggs and hard English cheeses. 'So we had dinner and she was a very nice girl with limited English.'

'The big drama in Burwash at the moment is that the Post Office in the newsagent has closed,' she wrote just after her sixtieth birthday, a couple of months before she died. 'I discovered it on Fri. when I needed to get some money. I had to go to Etchingham instead.' The Etchingham post office said it was just because the auditors were in, but 'now Tues. and no news. Mystery! It's going to cause chaos for the old-age pensioners and the mothers with child benefit. Nobody knows if it will reopen. The bus service will do well because not everybody drives.'

A few days later the situation still had not been resolved. Mum's informant phoned her a second time that day, telling her the same gossip. 'Poor old thing. I hope I don't go like that. I do keep my brain active so maybe not.'

This was her life, right to the end. Filled with little events, gossip, helping neighbours, cutting out recipes from magazines, phoning her sisters and daughters, writing letters, watering the garden and putting out seed for the birds.

Eleanor Clare Haynes died on 16 October 2002, aged sixty, on Oscar Wilde's birthday. She died in her sleep after an ordinary day following a busy fortnight looking after a friend's dog. She is buried at Burwash Church of St Lawrence. Her gravestone is topped with the carving of a daisy.

The words on her gravestone read:

In Loving Memory of Eleanor Clare Haynes
10 August 1942–16 October 2002

Tread lightly, she is near
Under the snow,
Speak gently, she can hear
The daisies grow.

SEVEN

EPILOGUE

On the third anniversary of my mother's death, I made a special meal and cleared the dining table of its day-to-day debris. We lit a new candle and put nasturtiums in a shallow dish with tea lights. I got out Mum's cut-glass wine glasses and bought a special bottle of French wine. A Beaujolais Villages. It's strange to think of all the things that go on in people's days: some are with family, nagging about untidy rooms and piles of washing-up, others are doing something special—a holiday, going to see a play, some are sick in hospital. Some go about their day not knowing it's their last. Some will receive good news of a competition win, or a job acceptance. Some will receive news of a death.

I think about Mum a lot, but I've decided to make a point of remembering her, with the family, with a special meal and good wine. She always made an effort with cooking and Peter remembers her getting out a good red wine for him whenever we came for lunch. I told the children we'd make the table nice to remember Grandma. I made a recipe that I'd cut out of a magazine: Italian meatballs cooked in tomatoes. Felix helped chop the bread soaked in milk. 'Do you know why we're having meatballs, Harry?' he ran into the sitting room where Harry was reading the second to last Deltora Quest book. 'To remember Grandma!'

Once I'd pried Felix off Harry's computer game, he played some violin, looking incredibly sweet in his blue undies and 'Mother's Worry' Mambo hand-me-down T-shirt: 'Go Tell Aunt Rhody', 'O Come Little Children', 'Twinkle Twinkle', 'Lightly Row' and 'Allegro'.

In the morning the boys and I had cleaned the Scout Hall. It was our turn. We popped over the road to say hello to long-time friends, Jane and Michael. I had a cup of tea and admired their tadpoles. Felix stayed to play with Kathleen and Harry ran home. Peter turned up as I was leaving, so the two of us had coffee and cake at Fireworks Cafe before he went to his office and I headed home to clean the bathroom.

It rained in the afternoon. Harry took his book into the car to read. 'I love the sound of the rain on the roof.' I took him a 'plane' meal: sausage omelette, crusty bread with butter and a fruit kebab stick.

I returned the scout key, cycling over with it to a lady's house in Thirroul, and did some shopping. Michael had returned with Felix and was having a glass of red wine with Peter in the garden.

These were some of the happenings in our ordinary day that happened too to be the anniversary of Mum's death. After the meal I watched some programs on SBS about Oscar Wilde. It was his 150th birthday, if that's quite the right way to say it. A number of actors, writers, broadcasters and musicians voiced quotes from Wilde, including the lines, 'Tread lightly, she is near,/Under the snow/Speak gently, she can hear/The daisies grow.' I prickled slightly as the words were spoken.

When someone dies, they do not disappear from your life. I will always be thinking of Mum. She's interwoven into the fabrics and cords of my life.

When I saw her gravestone for the first time, four years after she died, I felt a well of sadness again. But by the time I'd gone back with Máire, then again in the dark to plant bulbs, it was good to be doing something for her, and I felt she'd have liked the scene. Scrambling in the dark, pushing crocus and snowdrop bulbs into the grass, tight against the stone so they might survive a mower. Peter scattered some daisy seeds. The church clock struck one bell.

In the last stages of writing this, I remembered an old suitcase I had of letters. Unlike my mother, I do not throw out letters. I couldn't tell you for sure where the last decade's are, but a few decades' worth are in this suitcase, starting with letters from primary school friends written to me after the occasional sick day off school. Were there any letters from Mum and Dad? Of course there were, I just hadn't had the occasion to look at them again. So I sorted through the case, picking out theirs—looking for information about the life they and we all used to lead. Then I sorted them into eras: Egypt, Houston, back in Kent and, as far as Mum's went, Burwash, the last phase of her life.

It was a strange experience going through them. It brought back my tumultuous twenties to a disturbingly vivid degree. How much more emotionally serene my life was now, I couldn't help thinking. I could also see more clearly the sweep of both my own life and my mother's. The phases and eras that seem so final, absolute, and the essence of life itself, yet which yield to another.

They jogged the memory and also, from time to time,

corrected it. My memory told me Mum had not returned to England for her mother's funeral, when she was living in Cairo. It seemed odd to me as it wasn't that far to go—only a five-hour plane trip. But there it is in blue ink, in my father's handwriting:

> Mum got back safely last week after the funeral—she is upset from time to time when she is reminded of her Mum. The other day we got a letter from Sheila that had been delayed in the post for some time. It was written before Granny Mac died. Sheila was saying how much worse she was and that she didn't think she would last out for very much longer. That upset Mum a lot.

I light the fire in our weatherboard cottage, tying the newspaper in knots, like Mum showed me. The kindling wood spits and hisses and whips the fire into a yellow-orange life. Then the heat builds up and the fireplace becomes a mass of glowing red sticks.

I reflect how this house has brought me earth, fire and water. I'm closer to these ancient elements. My thumbs are far from green, but a little more often they are brown with earth. I see water almost every day. It's a different colour, mood ... And in the summer I'm in the water most days, swimming among the fish, swimming in the salty water means a shower when I return; our golden fish flash in the big fish tank in the sitting room: water in my life.

Mum would 'approve' of this life out of the city. She'd be pleased we have so many friends, especially ones with children, families we can get together with: local music events, camping under the stars with some, taking long cycle rides with others. I'd tell her about Peter's gardening efforts, how the snake beans did so well last year, how he's put nets up against the satin bowerbirds.

One night, not long ago, there was a lunar eclipse. We watched a blotting-paper moon soak up a purple shadow, curved to the shape of the Earth. As it crept up the white disc, it took on a smoky orange glow, and for a while it looked so round. I thought of Mum preparing for the solar eclipse.

Reading the letters I am struck at how I find myself responding to so much more than the words. After all, words only ever reveal part of the story. When I read a letter from a certain era, it's like I am dropped back there and a part of my mind responds by conjuring up the emotional backdrop. I sense—or remember—all over again the details that aren't in writing. Whether annoyance, plain busyness or boredom; my reluctance to visit Houston, for example.

There's the voice—not just perhaps hearing the voice in my head—but the tone and the background to that tone, which is a lifetime of living with that person, who, when you're a child, is a giant.

The word 'Houston' conjures up a bleakness and blandness that must be more to do with the family situation there than the place itself. But then, when I think of the places where Mum was happy, and especially that last era of her life in Burwash—she was happiest in a community. The village suited her—as where I'm living now suits me. Houston was large scale, you didn't often bump into people you knew, there wasn't the expat community that there was in Egypt.

If Houston had a soul, she certainly didn't find it.

There's much more feeling in her letters from Burwash. Her health was on a knife edge but she had connection and community, and, finally, self-determination.

In the shuffling of stuff in our last move, I came across a notebook where I'd occasionally made diary-like entries. I found a few paragraphs I'd written after a phone conversation with my mother.

A few weeks ago my mother called me and told me she'd been advised to have a heart transplant.

Without one, the specialist said, she had a year to
live. 'I thought maybe I had two,' she told him.
I've spoken to her twice since that call. The last time
was last night. She'd been expecting to hear from
Harefield Hospital calling her up for a series of tests.
She rang the specialists and asked what was
happening. 'I've just typed the letter to your doctor
and they'll be posted on Monday,' the secretary told
her. (This was two weeks after she'd seen the
specialist.) 'I've already lost a month. Now I've only
got eleven months,' my mother said to the woman,
urging her to hurry things up.

She said: 'Sometimes I think of going up there for the
operation and I think, I'm terrified, then I think, no
you're not, you're just being silly.'

I told her I planned to come over in September.
'That's interesting,' she said. 'I was thinking that if I
started to go downhill, if I've got a year, then at some
point I'll start going downhill, then I'd pay for you
and Harry to come out.'

'I think about my life,' she said, 'and I like it. It's
not the way I thought it would be but I like the fact
I've finished my sheep embroidery and got it framed
on the wall. I like that I can sit in the garden, and I
live in a beautiful house and have all my beautiful

things around me. I like my life—I'd just like it to go on a bit longer.'

One year a friend asked me if it was difficult facing Christmas, thinking of my mother. I explained that she was in my thoughts and part of our lives but was now a lighter presence, like a fluttering kite at the end of a long string as we walk along the beach. My feelings are not as raw and I don't feel as sad as I did when she first died, but every now and then I feel her tug.

ACKNOWLEDGMENTS

Thank you to the staff at Murdoch Books for their encouragement in bringing this manuscript to print, particularly Diana Hill and Kay Scarlett, for their faith early on, and also Desney Shoemark for her friendly and professional support throughout. Many thanks to editor, Karen Ward for a sympathetic and sensitive touch. Thanks too, to friends who listened and several who read extracts, particularly Jenny Davis, Karen Fisher and Jude Crichton; to members of my family who helped with family history, especially Máire Carr and Sheila McGonigle—any errors are mine.